THE I

The Play
of
The Silver Sword

STUART HENSON

from the novel by
IAN SERRAILLIER

HEINEMANN
EDUCATIONAL

Heinemann Educational Publishers
Halley Court, Jordan Hill, Oxford OX2 8EJ
A Division of Reed Educational & Professional Publishing Ltd

MELBOURNE   AUCKLAND   FLORENCE   PRAGUE
MADRID   ATHENS   SINGAPORE   TOKYO
SAO PAULO   CHICAGO   PORTSMOUTH (NH)   MEXICO
IBADAN   GABORONE   JOHANNESBURG
KAMPALA   NAIROBI

97 98 17 16 15 14 13 12 11 10

ISBN 0 435 23407 2

Printed in England by Athenæum Press Ltd,
Gateshead, Tyne & Wear

A NOTE ON THE ADAPTATION AND PRODUCTION

by Stuart Henson

The Silver Sword is an epic tale. The children's journey to reunite the pieces of their shattered world, their struggle to restore the family whole, strikes a deep chord in most young readers. It has the stuff of myth in it and the urgency of our need to establish order in the face of confusion and hostility. There is danger and warmth, loss and discovery, humour and sorrow. The novel presents an essentially dramatic story, but in order to realise it on the stage, some of the original has to be excluded.

This script does not attempt to reproduce the reader's experience as film or television might do. To be realistic and inclusive was not our aim. Our touchstone was fidelity to the spirit of the original. Our intent was to make a play, fast-moving and episodic in structure, which would work in the tradition of Brecht's 'epic' or 'open' theatre. The choice of the 'epic' mode seemed the obvious one, allowing as it does, freedom from the constraints of verisimilitude, the energy and humour of 'rough theatre' and immediate contact with the audience.

The original plan was to play our story on a simple 'thrust' stage, with the actors and musicians not involved in a scene watching and waiting on either side. As rehearsal progressed, however, it became apparent that the play demanded so many props and stretched our military costume resources so far, that it would be more satisfactory to allow the actors to prepare themselves out of the audience's view. The compromise was to use a proscenium stage with a thrust of similar size in which three key areas were isolated by spotlighting:

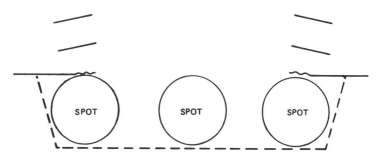

Our first link with the audience was the narrator for each part of the story, who watched the action from one of the 'spots' right, or left. He (they, in the case of the children in the first part) remained lit throughout, except in those scenes which require total darkness on the stage. A packing crate sufficed for a seat for the narrator and he stood to address the audience. The narrator held a book, a script, to tell the story from, and thus was able to act as prompt from the earliest rehearsal. These simple conventions seemed quite acceptable to our audience, though the narrator was often very close to the action.

I chose to attempt the first production with the smallest possible cast — twenty-five — emphasising that it was a 'team' presentation involving most of the actors in about five roles each with minor changes of costume — hats, coats, shawls etc. There were half a dozen 'principal' roles though, which could not be confused. The children, the parents and Jan, had to be the exclusive responsibility of one actor throughout. I see no reason why a cast of a hundred could not be used, each playing one role. Most directors will opt, I think, for a number somewhere between. The narrator's role was split among three characters: Edek,

Joseph and Ivan. I have kept to this here because it seemed to work well. The narrator is thus half way between actor and character — a little alienation device — but I can envisage a production in which the narration is spoken by a separate storyteller or 'singer' as in the *Caucasian Chalk Circle*.

It did not take the actors long to stop worrying about the illusion of reality. A pile of rubble dragged in on sacking, half a dozen straw bales, a couple of tea-chests, a fireplace, a signpost, a table with a typewriter — these are the settings. In most instances the actor could literally pick up his 'set' and walk off with it. The fireplace and the signal were clipped to part of a mobile scaffold tower. This had the advantage of being easily whisked away into the wings at the end of the scene and allowed Joseph to climb up the chimney and Jan and Edek to mount the signal gantry. On some stages, more permanent features would have to be constructed. We were also fortunate in having mobile staging on which to present the escape over the roofs. Many productions will, I imagine, keep a permanent raised area upstage, using it again in the lakeside scene at the end of the play. Back projection or screen projection of transparencies would be a valuable additional way of realising a number of the various settings.

I believe the play is flexible enough to work on almost any stage, though in the text I have retained much of the original direction with regard to entrances, exits and the location of scenes. I hope this may help some users, especially those who are simply reading the play, but many directors will wish to alter them to suit their theatres and productions.

The use of music is another area in which each new production will find its own way. Music is an integral part of the 'epic' style of presentation. There are four songs: the prisoners' 'welcome' to Joseph, Edek's song, the refugees' round song and the closing song. Accompaniment for each of these, and for the peasant dance, would be the minimum requirement. No doubt directors will find other opportunities, such as scene changes, to make use of their musicians. Ideally, the musicians would also be members of the cast. In the original production the music had an Eastern European flavour and was scored for three or four wind instruments and percussion.

A play of this nature must move at considerable speed: the actors are bound to a high degree of team-discipline and alertness. Scene changing, for instance, was managed entirely by the actors in our production. Responsibility for the many properties lay in their hands also. The efficient exchange of a uniform greatcoat or a military helmet between scenes was vital. It is difficult to impress upon a cast of eleven, twelve and thirteen-year-olds the importance of backstage drill, but if the script is demanding in this respect the rewards come later. After eight weeks of strenuous rehearsal, the extra effort of concentration bears fruit: energy, commitment and an air of purpose characterise the performance.

In our production, the actors were given the additional task of preparing a number of short sections of the performance themselves. In the text I have numbered these as *improvisations* for that is how they began. Each is keyed back into the script with a prescribed ending, but the participants devise their own action and dialogue. Sometimes in the rush of rehearsal, we had to short-cut the process somewhat by allowing the actors concerned to get together and write a miniature script for their so-called improvisation. On the other hand, some just grew with confidence into quite scene-stealing contributions.

I am aware that many of the young actors who come to the play with a particular affection for the novel will find things missing. Bistro, the chimpanzee, and Ludwig, the dog, do not appear. Directors who have already had to audition for a cockerel and grey cat will appreciate why.

The escape in the canoes is omitted also. There is a certain amount of new material, as in the opening scenes, but much of the dialogue will be instantly familiar. I hope this script will provide an opportunity for such readers to actively 'take part' in a favourite story.

I am grateful to Ian Serraillier for his support in the project, his advice and suggestions. I must also acknowledge the contribution of the first cast at Kimbolton School who built the play, scene by scene, with me.

LIST OF CHARACTERS

EDEK
RUTH
BRONIA
JOSEPH
SCHOOLCHILDREN
TRUDI
ANDREZ
ANNA
SARA
GERMAN SOLDIERS
COMMANDANT
PRISONERS
PEASANT
PEASANT WIFE
MRS KRAUSE
JAN
MARGRIT
PEASANT II
MARKET CROWD
EVA
KATE
IVAN
RUSSIAN LIEUTENANT
REFUGEES

REFUGEE WIFE
RUSSIAN SOLDIERS
SECRETARY
DOCTOR
ORDERLY
REGISTRAR
RELIEF OFFICER
COOK
ASSISTANT
MRS BOROWICZ
RAGGED BOY
U.S. MILITARY POLICEMAN
CAPTAIN GREENWOOD
LIEUTENANT JAMES
G.I.
CORPORAL
FARMER
LABOURERS
MAN ON BICYCLE
WOMAN WITH BARROW
JOE
FRENCH DOCTOR
SUPERINTENDENT
NURSE
SWISS PEOPLE

SYNOPSIS OF SCENES

ACT ONE

1	Warsaw: A Schoolroom
2	Zakyna Prison
3	'The Cooler'
4	A Peasant's House
5	The City
6	The City

ACT TWO

1	The Balickis' House
2	The Cellar
3	A Croft and a Marketplace
4	The Cellar
5	A Russian Control Post
6	The Cellar

ACT THREE

1	The Crossroads
2	A Field Kitchen
3	On the Road to Switzerland
4	An American Military Court
5	On the Road
6	On the Road
7	On the Road
8	A Red Cross Camp
9	The Shore of Lake Constance
10	A Cabin on the Steamer and Appenzell Village

ACT ONE

Scene 1

As the audience enters the house lights are low. Stage is half-lit. Technical checks and last minute adjustments are being made by the players. They are busy, confident. They ignore the audience. One or two rehearse with musical instruments.

House lights down. Spot intensifies centre. EDEK, *who has been leafing through the narrator's script, nods to* STAGE MANAGER *and walks into spot centre, looks firmly around the audience before speaking.*

EDEK (*as narrator*): Welcome! We are here to tell a story. You have come to see, to listen, to understand. We thank you.

Our story is one story and many stories. It is my story. It is my father's story. It is the story of a Polish family and of what happened to them in the Second World War.

Our home was in a suburb of Warsaw where my father, Joseph Balicki, was headmaster of a primary school. In 1940 Warsaw was a place of terror. When the Nazis took away our father I was eleven, Ruth was thirteen and Bronia was not old enough to understand.

Pause. RUTH *and* BRONIA *join him in the spotlight. In the half stage light the actors set up a blackboard, benches and desks. A picture of Hitler is hung on the blackboard. The children move to sit on packing cases at narrator's spot point L and watch while stage lights rise to full.*

Hear now the story of Joseph Balicki. Hear why he was taken to prison. Hear how he escaped. Hear how he returned to Warsaw!

JOSEPH *is teaching, reading from the Bible, in German*

JOSEPH: Stehe auf und numm das Kindlein und seine Mutter zu dir und flieh nach Ägyptenland . . .
(*Pause*) Carry on please Trudi.

TRUDI (*starts guiltily, stands slowly and begins to read clumsily in German. JOSEPH corrects her errors but eventually she can go no further.*): Und er stand auf . . . und nahm das Kindlein . . . und seine Mutter . . . zu sich bei der Nacht . . . und entwich nach . . . Ägyptenland.

JOSEPH: Andrez.

ANDREZ (*stands, begins and stumbles just as badly*): Und blieb allda bis nach dem Tod des Herodes, auf dass . . . erfüllet würde . . . (*He looks up and pleads*) Mr. Balicki, why do we have to read in German? None of us understands a word. It doesn't make any sense to us. (*Pause*) How can we learn anything if we don't know what we're saying?

JOSEPH: Sit down Andrez! (*Tight lipped*) You know very well. It is decreed by Hitler that all Polish Primary Schools will use German as their first language.

ANDREZ (*who has not obeyed the command to sit, thrashes the book down on the desk*): I HATE GERMAN. I hate their animal language. The Nazis shot my brother. He hated them. *He* wouldn't ever have licked their boots! (*He storms out of the classroom concealing his tears.*)

JOSEPH: Wait . . . Andrez . . . (*Pause*) He will come back. We must try to understand how much it hurts for him . . . (*Pause*) Anna, continue please.

ANNA (*stands and begins to read, deliberately stupidly*): Da Herodes nun sah . . . dass er von den Weisen . . . betrogen war . . . ward er sehr . . . zornig . . . und schickte aus . . .

JOSEPH: Stop! (*Long pause — he is struggling with himself. Then, deliberately*) Anna, Sara, the Polish Bibles please!

(*Silently the children pass round the Bibles. The German ones are collected. The whole class is very subdued.* ANNA *is last to take her place and looks up at* JOSEPH *who smiles, turns to the blackboard and with a simple, quiet movement faces the picture of Hitler to the wall*) What he does not see and cannot hear will not grieve his heart.

He nods to ANNA; *she finds the page (Matthew 2. v16—) and reads in her native language, very clearly, with a ringing quality in her voice. (Throughout the play, words that would have spoken in Polish are spoken in English.) The other children are looking at her, not at the books. Suddenly she stops in mid-sentence.*

Enter two GERMAN SOLDIERS *and* COMMANDANT *(L), forcing the sullen* ANDREZ *in front of them. They stand motionless in the doorway. The* COMMANDANT *looks slowly round the classroom. His eyes rest on the books.*

SOLDIER (*yells, suddenly*): Aufstehen! (*The class leap to attention*)

COMMANDANT *strides across to the picture and flicks it over with his baton.*

Blackout 5 seconds.

Scene 2

Zakyna Prison. The PRISONERS *are stamping round the exercise yard, arms folded, blowing hands, flapping — anything to keep warm. Floor standing lights play on their faces. Intermittent sound of dog barking. Under their breath they are muttering, almost chanting one word 'cold'. After a minute,* JOSEPH *is pushed into the centre by* TWO GUARDS. *He stands abjectly.*

3

PRISONERS:

> Welcome, brother to Zakyna
> Hotel for your winter holiday.
> The management is glad to have you with us
> And sincerely hope that you'll enjoy your stay.

PRISONER 1 (*speaks*):

> Picture postcard scenery! Pine trees . . .
> Snow . . . Barbed wire!

PRISONERS:

> You may not want a ten year booking
> Unfortunately there are no trains home.
> Last week one guest ran off to find one:
> They say they let the guard dogs chew his bones!

PRISONER 2 (*speaks*):

> See the bright lights! (*Searchlight*)
> Regular firework display! (*Machine gun*)

PRISONERS:

> Every room here is air-conditioned:
> The wind blows in the windows and the doors.
> You can always take a bath when it's not frozen
> And when it rains there's water on each floor.

PRISONER 3 (*speaks*):

> Mountain air! Works wonders!
> Bronchitis! Pneumonia!
> Kills all known diseases — you too if you're not careful.

PRISONERS:

> The food simply defies description:
> It's the best that Hitler's kitchens can provide.
> Even the soup's so thin and hungry
> It tries to eat your stomach from inside!
>> *Pantomime: running to the latrine.*

Improvisation I: *Two prisoners clown a waiter and customer sketch. In the end customer chooses cabbage
soup and does a 'waiter-there's-a-fly-in-my-soup' gag.
The other prisoners howl and carry him off protesting.*
JOSEPH *remains seated C looking at photos.*

4

EDEK (*as narrator*): Zakyna lay in the mountains of South Poland — a few wooden huts clinging to the bleak hillside. Day and night the wind beat down on them, for the pine trees were thin and gave little shelter. Snow smothered the huts. It gave a coating of white fur to the twelve foot double fence of wire that surrounded the clearing. In stormy weather it blew into the bare huts through the cracks in the walls. There was no comfort in Zakyna.

    For two winters Joseph was ill: he had neither the strength nor spirit to escape. In the summer between, six of them broke out — but they were caught.

COMMANDANT'S VOICE: Punishment, one month solitary confinement.

EDEK: But still by the second spring, Joseph had made his plan. The nights were growing warmer. This time he was alone. He would not fail!

Improvisation II: *Inspection time:* JOSEPH *flicks pellets at the guard and is taken to the cooler. Ends with* COMMANDANT *shouting sentence of punishment.*

COMMANDANT: Joseph Balicki; insulting misconduct. Seven days solitary confinement!

Scene 3

    The cooler, an isolated area upstage. White light from above.

EDEK (*narrates*): For two days he stamped up and down to keep himself warm. He dared not lie down for more than a few minutes at a time in case he dropped off to sleep and never woke again. Twice a day the guard brought him food. For the rest of the time he was alone.

Improvisation III: JOSEPH *steals keys and uniform from* GUARD. *Ends with sound of guards shouting, off right. Trumpet blows roll call.* GUARDS *fall in raggedly downstage but stiffen to attention when* COMMANDANT

enters and surveys the line. JOSEPH *has joined the line,
falling in last.* COMMANDANT *counts under his breath
and then begins to walk down the line. The* SOLDIERS
*relax and stamp or beat their arms. This is tedious
routine and it's cold.*

COMMANDANT (*to first guard*): 'zu melden?

GUARD: 'in Ordnung.

>*As* COMMANDANT *passes along the line each* GUARD
including JOSEPH *mutters the same reply.*

COMMANDANT: Wegtreten!

>*They fall out in twos and threes, swapping cigarettes,
mumbling, laughing coarsely; three more huddle centre
right.* JOSEPH *walks past them; one grabs his shoulders.*

GUARD I: Wohin gehen Sie?

JOSEPH (*shrugs*): Shangri La.

GUARD II: Wer war denn das?

GUARD III: 'weiss nicht. Hans vielleicht.

>JOSEPH *exits quickly down right.*

Scene 4

>*The stage is in darkness, a torch is seen. A* PEASANT
*is gathering wood from a pile. He hears a noise and
flashes round, shining the beam into the audience.*

PEASANT: Who's there? (*Silence*) Who's there? (*Silence*)
Damned rats!

>*The torch beam turns.* JOSEPH *approaches in dark-
ness right.* PEASANT *whistles nervously;* JOSEPH *joins
in and finishes the tune.* PEASANT *turns the torch on
his face.*

JOSEPH (*steadily*): I have you covered with my pistol. If
you make a move I'll shoot.

PEASANT: Beggar me!

JOSEPH: Be quiet! Do you want me to shoot? Hand me
your torch! (*He seizes it from the trembling hands and
shines it on him.*) Are you Polish?

PEASANT: Yes corporal . . . er captain . . .

JOSEPH (*more gently*): Do as I tell you and you'll come to no harm. Do you live here? (PEASANT *nods*) Take me inside!

Lights up on peasant croft interior: two boxes for seats by hearth. PEASANT'S WIFE *is polishing a pot.*

JOSEPH (*throwing greatcoat over a box*): Here's the pistol I almost shot you with! It's a slab of chocolate. (*He breaks it into three.* PEASANTS *wait suspiciously until he eats before swallowing theirs.*)

PEASANT: I don't understand. You look like a Pole. You speak like a Pole. But your uniform. . . . (*Sound of bell, distant.*)

JOSEPH: That's the prison bell. It's a long time since it rang like that — when the last prisoner escaped.

WIFE: You've come to search for him?

JOSEPH: I am the prisoner. I knocked out the guard and stole his uniform. Look if you don't believe me, here's my convict's number burnt into my arm. (*Pause*) I want you to hide me!

PEASANT *and* WIFE *turn heads to one another, freeze.*

EDEK (*narrator*): That night Joseph slept in a warm bed for the first time in two years.

In the morning the old man went to work as usual. They arranged a danger signal. They knew if they were found hiding him they would die, but they were brave people and did not hesitate.

EDEK *turns toward peasant croft interior.* JOSEPH *in shirt sleeves, washing in bowl.*

PEASANT: Very good! I must go now. If there are soldiers coming across in the mountain lift I shall whistle, three times (*demonstrates*) O.K.?

JOSEPH (*drying on towel*): Thank you!

PEASANT: You will have time to get to the woodshed. The hiding-place is well concealed. My wife will stack timber over the entrance. They will not find you there. (WIFE *nods*) Goodbye my friend!

JOSEPH: Goodbye — and thank you again.

PEASANT: We would do the same always. Every prisoner is someone's son. (*Exit*)

WIFE: Our own son — he is your age — he was fighting in Kalisz. We have not heard from him for seven months.

JOSEPH *looks at the peasant woman. Sympathy and sorrow move him to speak but he can say nothing. Seeing it has struck a sombre note, the* WIFE *changes the subject, bustling to the window with the bowl, folding the towel.*

WIFE: You have children of your own? It is a long time too since you have seen them?

JOSEPH (*sits slowly, takes wallet and photos from greatcoat pocket*): Yes, Mother, I have three children. They were in Warsaw. I do not know what has become of them.

WIFE (*crosses to stand behind* JOSEPH): Oh, they're fine upright children. The smallest, she's so pretty! What is she called?

JOSEPH: That is my Bronia. This is Ruth. Edek is the middle one. He is very serious, very determined. You can see he does not smile very often, but when he does . . .

This is my wife. See how Ruth is like her. Ruth will be a teacher one day — a great teacher I think. Not like me. I am not a learned man. I work in the primary school in the East Side of the city. At least, I *did* work. I was taken by the Secret Police. We read our lessons in Polish.

WIFE: I understand.

JOSEPH (*looks down at photo again*): Ruth reads all the time. Everything. Anything. She is a true scholar. But this war . . .

There is no food in Warsaw. Everyone is afraid. You can see fear hiding in people's eyes. Sometimes I think you can even *smell* fear. It's like a fog. People no longer live their own lives. There are few families that have stayed together now in Warsaw.

Sudden loud, strident knocking.

COMMANDANT: Open! Open! Quick or you'll pay!

JOSEPH *grabs coat and hat and starts towards the door. Turns, helpless.*

WIFE: No time! There was no whistle! (*She looks around, sees the chimney*) Quick — up there! There's an opening on the right, halfway up!

JOSEPH *climbs up into the chimney. Noise of door being forced.* TWO GUARDS *tumble in.*

GUARD I: That man at the cage. He is your husband?

WIFE: Yes!

GUARD I (*laughs*): Insolent old beggar. I taught him a lesson! Look after him when he comes home — if he can walk!

WIFE *cries.*

Improvisation IV: *They search the house. Ends with both about to leave.* GUARD II *turns to* WIFE.

GUARD II: What you snivelling for, tramp!

GUARD I: You'll snivel if you're hiding a military prisoner!

GUARD II (*looks up at the hearth*): What about the chimney? Plenty of room to hide up there!

WIFE: Plenty of soot too!

GUARD I: Then we'll send a bullet up for luck!

Shot and sootfall. GUARDS *scarper, dusting their uniforms.* JOSEPH, *dazed and shaken, half falls down from chimney.* WIFE *supports him to a seat.* PEASANT *appears in doorway. He is beaten up.*

PEASANT: I'm sorry, I didn't have time to warn you. They hid themselves in the cage. I didn't see them till it was too late!

Blackout 5 seconds.

Scene 5

As EDEK, *the narrator speaks, the scene is set for*
'The City': piles of bricks; a makeshift street sign;
various tent-like constructions, some with stoves;
families clustered round; people crossing, waving,
gossiping, arguing. . . . JOSEPH *stands in the same*
place as last scene. He looks bewildered.

EDEK : In the country war rolled at a distance: grief came
from the distance. The postman brought a letter. Sometimes the letter never came: then sorrow grew slowly.
The peasants were hungry. But they could not remember
a winter when they were not hungry. In the country life
was still the same.

In the city it was different.

Four weeks and a half Joseph walked. In four weeks
and a half he arrived in Warsaw. It was not the Warsaw
he knew.

The place was bleak and silent as the craters of the
moon. Instead of proud homes he found crumbling
walls; instead of streets, tracks of rubble between
mountains of bricks. Windows stared, charred and
glassless.

Yet in this wilderness people went on living, wander-
ing, pale, hungry-eyed, vanishing down paths among
ruins. They had made their homes in cellars or had dug
caves in the rubble. A bomb-gash in a cellar wall was
draped bright with curtains. In another hole, a window-
box of purple crocuses. Here and there a tree that had
escaped the blast sprouted spring leaves.

Improvisation V: JOSEPH *begins to ask after his street —*
family — children — someone he knew. Finally someone
points to a pile of rubble. He walks to it (C), and picks
up a brick. He stands a long time numbed with despair.
MRS KRAUSE *hangs up a sign on her house R.* JOSEPH
walks slowly over to it and reads: 'Polish Welfare'.

MRS KRAUSE *is sitting at a makeshift desk.* JOSEPH *waits. She finishes writing and looks up.*

MRS KRAUSE (*half interested*): Yes?

JOSEPH: I would like to make an enquiry about my family. (*Pause*)

MRS KRAUSE: Yes?

JOSEPH: They have been missing — perhaps two years.

MRS KRAUSE: Name?

JOSEPH: I am Joseph Balicki, schoolmaster.

MRS KRAUSE: Where do you live? (JOSEPH *looks down*) Where *did* you live?

JOSEPH *turns towards the pile of rubble.*

JOSEPH: Before the war, that was our house.

MRS KRAUSE: Wait a minute — I know you. Was your school in the Eastern Quarter? My daughter went there, years back. She pointed you out when you moved here. I know your wife quite well. We used to queue together. (*She offers him a seat.*) The Nazis destroyed your school.

JOSEPH: What happened to my wife?

MRS KRAUSE: They came for her in the night, in January last year. It was just after Dr. Frank called for a million foreign workers to go to Germany. She's in Germany, probably working on the land. I'm a member of the Polish Council for Protection and we tried to trace her, but without success.

JOSEPH: And the children — did they go with her?

MRS KRAUSE (*looks down*): I don't know anything about them.

JOSEPH: Tell me.

MRS KRAUSE: I know nothing.

JOSEPH: That's not true. As a member of the Council, you must have found out something.

MRS KRAUSE: On the night your wife was taken away, someone fired at the van from the attic of your house. A tyre was punctured and one of the Nazi soldiers was hit in the arm. But they got away with the van all the

11

same. An hour later they sent a truckload of soldiers with explosives. They blew up the whole place. The children have not been seen since.

JOSEPH *stands without a word. Turns, walks to Centre. His face is stony. After a long pause* MRS KRAUSE *follows him. Puts her hand out to his shoulder.*

MRS KRAUSE: You must have known something like this might happen. Did you never make any plans. Did you never fix a meeting place?

JOSEPH (*thinks for a moment*): Yes, as a matter of fact we did. We arranged that, if we were separated, we would try to make for Switzerland. My wife is Swiss and her parents live there still.

MRS KRAUSE (*kindly*): There's your answer, then. Go to Switzerland, and with God's help you will find her there.

JOSEPH: But the children — they may still be here.

MRS KRAUSE: It's no use your going on like this. The house was locked before the soldiers left; the children could not have survived the explosion. If you want to go on searching, search for your wife.

JOSEPH: Germany's a large place. What hope should I have of finding her?

MRS KRAUSE *has already turned back to her house: she turns to him once more.*

MRS KRAUSE: She might escape — you did. (*Exit*)

JOSEPH *squats despondently behind the pile of rubble, idly picking over the bricks.*

Scene 6

The stage light dim. One spot remains, isolating JOSEPH. *The city people disperse and exit in their own time.*

EDEK (*narrator*): He spent several more days looking for the children. One afternoon, while he was poking among the rubble of his old home, he found a tiny silver sword.

About five inches long, it had a brass hilt engraved with a dragon breathing fire. It was a paper knife that he had once given to his wife for a birthday present.

JOSEPH *stands, musing. He wipes the sword with care on the sleeve of his coat. He turns, suddenly aware he is being watched.* JAN, *who has entered silently, is squatting on the edge of the spotlight. He has his wooden 'treasure box' in one hand, in the other, a 'travelling box' with a bony grey kitten. Eyeing* JOSEPH *with suspicion,* JAN *turns to his box and lifts out his kitten, as if to say: 'You can't hurt us, we protect each other.' But* JOSEPH *smiles. He steps to him and strokes the kitten.*

JOSEPH (*gently*): What's his name?

JAN: He hasn't got a name. He's just mine.

JOSEPH *takes the kitten and holds him up admiringly. As he does so* JAN *slips a hand into* JOSEPH'S *coat pocket and lifts a wrapped sandwich.* JOSEPH *turns back.* JAN *conceals the theft.*

JOSEPH: What's *your* name?

JAN *pouts: turns away into the shadow; unwraps and sniffs the sandwich. After a second's thought he skips back close to* JOSEPH.

JAN: Will you give me that sword?

JOSEPH: But it's mine.

JAN: You found it on my pitch. This is my place.

JOSEPH (*sadly*): No, this is my house — at least this rubble is what's left of it.

JAN: I'll give you food for it. (*Offers* JOSEPH *the sandwich.*)

JOSEPH: No thanks, I have my own. (*Hand to pocket. Pause.*) You little thief!

JOSEPH *grabs at the sandwich, but he's holding the kitten.* JAN *steps back and munches at it.*

JOSEPH (*conciliatory*): Look, maybe you can help me.

JAN *looks suspicious, but pays attention. During the next speech he takes the kitten and returns it to its box.*

13

JOSEPH (*continuing*): I'm searching for my family — three children. (*Here he gives a brief description of the actors playing Edek, Ruth and Bronia. He shows the photograph, if he has time.*) We all lived here. I don't suppose you've seen anything of them.

JAN: Warsaw is full of lost children. They're dirty and starving and they all look alike. (*He turns, and is almost gone when JOSEPH calls him back.*)

JOSEPH: Wait! I'll give you this sword on one condition. (JAN *comes back*) I'm not sure that my children *are* dead. If ever you see Ruth or Edek or Bronia, you must tell them about our meeting. Tell them I'm going to Switzerland to find their mother. To their grandparents' home. Tell them to follow as soon as they can. (*Pause: JAN makes no response.*)

Now, listen. I'm starting off for Switzerland tonight. I don't want to walk all the way, so I'm going to jump a train. Where's the best place?

JAN *holds out his hand for the sword, takes it quickly and hides it in his 'treasure box'.*

JAN: You will be caught and shot. Or you will freeze to death in the trucks. The nights are bitter. Your hair will be white with frost. Your fingers will turn to icicles. And when the Nazis find you, you will be stiff as the boards at the bottom of the truck. That is what happens to those who jump trains.

JOSEPH: You seem to know a lot about it!

JAN: I've seen it.

JOSEPH: Can't be helped. I must risk it. It's better than going back to the place I've come from.

JAN: I'll take you to the bend where the trains slow down. We must go by the back ways — it's curfew time. If the Nazi patrols see us they'll shoot.

JOSEPH *struggles to keep up with* JAN *as he dashes from point to point in a zig-zag across the stage. Finally they rest, crouching breathless in a dim spot Right.*

JOSEPH (*after a long pause*): I have much to thank you for and I don't even know your name. (*Another long pause:* JAN *says nothing.*) Have you no parents?

JAN: All I have is my cat, and this box.

JOSEPH: You won't come with me?

JAN (*ignoring the question, opening his box and examining the sword*): This is the best of my treasures. It will bring me luck. And it will bring you luck because you gave it to me. (*Pause*) I don't usually tell people my name — it's not safe. But because you gave me the sword, I'll tell you. It's Jan.

JOSEPH: There are many Jans in Poland. What's your surname?

JAN: That's all. Just Jan.

Sound of slow train approaching. JOSEPH *stands, looks out into the darkness, back to* JAN.

JOSEPH: Goodbye Jan. Remember your promise. Whatever happens, I shall not forget you.

Blackout. The train sound builds to a climax, and fades slowly.

ACT TWO

Scene 1

Spot right. JOSEPH *walks into spot and addresses audience directly.*

JOSEPH (*now narrator*): What had happened to my family that night when the storm troopers called at the house? Was Mrs Krause's story true? Did they take away my wife? Did they return and blow up the house with the children in it?

Hear now what did happen.

Lights up to half on raised stage C. One strong blue/white beam suggests moonlight. RUTH, BRONIA *and* EDEK *sitting up.* EDEK *hugging his knees to his chest.* RUTH *has arm around* BRONIA.

JOSEPH (*continues*): That night there was an inch of snow on the roofs of Warsaw. The children's room was on the top floor, below the attic. They woke to unfamiliar sounds . . .

EDEK *listens, ear to floor. Two* GERMAN SOLDIERS *march* MARGRIT *across the front of stage, L–R. They pass briefly through one of the downstage spots, which fades in and out as the following dialogue begins and ends. The three figures are seen for only a moment, just long enough for the audience to register* MARGRIT, *and what is happening. It is important that the children do not* see *this themselves: they can only* hear *what is going on below them. If it is possible, the two areas of light should be separate. The voices are heard before and after the figures are seen.*

FIRST SOLDIER: Mantel und Papier mitbringen! Verstanden?

MARGRIT: What do you mean? I don't understand. I'm sorry, I can't leave the house . . .

SECOND SOLDIER: Still! Schnell. Wir haben keine Zeit. Was ist denn los?

MARGRIT: My children! They're upstairs. They won't know where —

FIRST SOLDIER: Die Kinder? Nein. Die kommen nicht mit. Lass' sie doch!

MARGRIT: But don't you see? Their father isn't here. They'll be alone. I can't leave my children. . . .

EDEK (*suddenly, violently*): Stop you bastards. Stop! LEAVE MY MOTHER ALONE!

He moves like a cat up to the highest level and swings down with a roll of felt. Sound of: engine starting; doors; van driving away. EDEK *is at the window with a rifle. He fires twice.* BRONIA *is crying.* RUTH *is almost in tears herself. They move close to* EDEK. *He is staring through the window. He too would cry, but he is a member of the Warsaw Boys Rifle Brigade.*

EDEK (*still staring*): I hit one of the swine.

RUTH: That was very silly of you. They'll come back for us now. We must get away from here before they do.

EDEK (*quietly*): I couldn't let them take Mother away like that.

RUTH: There's no time to waste. (*She fetches coats, hats and boots which they put on over their pyjamas. She helps* BRONIA, *who is still sobbing.*)

EDEK (*rather harshly*): Stop howling Bronia. It won't help. (*Pause*) We can't get out the front way. There's another van coming. I heard the whistle.

RUTH: What about the back?

EDEK: The wall's too high. We'd never get Bronia over. And there are Nazis billeted in that street. There's only one way — over the roof.

RUTH: We'll never manage that!

BRONIA: I can hear them coming. Ruth, I can hear them coming! Where's Mother?

EDEK: It's the only way. Through the attic trapdoor. You'll have to climb Bronia. And listen: if you make a sound we shall never see Mother again. We shall all be killed.

RUTH: Of course we shall see her again. But only if you do as Edek says.

They climb up on the roof, helping BRONIA *who clings to* EDEK'S *rifle.* RUTH *is last. They crouch, gasping in the cold. Lights fade on all but roof, which is moonlit from directly above.*

EDEK: If we can make it to the V between the chimney and the roof ridge, we'll be all right. We can scale along the terrace. They'll never see us from the street.

Sound of cars; a string of commands; doors. A flashing light.

EDEK: I'll go first. I can't carry you Bron, but all you have to do is jump to me when you get over the parapet. Try to grab that telephone bracket. I'll catch you as you land.

They jump, one by one, out into the darkness. As RUTH *goes the last white light blacks out. Only the flashing light continues.*

(Pause)

JOSEPH:
Go quickly, young ones, frightened ones,
Into the black night,
Into the foreign night,

Go safely, young ones, shaken ones,
Over the cold roofs,
Over the slippery roofs.

Go far from this place.
Go where you are not sought.

Go quickly.
Go together.
The night is full of sounds
That speak danger.
The night is full of
Flames.

Go bravely, young ones.
Your childhood will soon be no more
Than rubble on the ground.
Explosion. Blackout.

Scene 2

> *The cellar.* RUTH *and* BRONIA *set up box furniture.*
> RUTH *sits and begins to match two tatty ends of cur-*
> *tain.* BRONIA *is rather sadly admiring her charcoal*
> *drawings which decorate the walls. One figure has a*
> *grin. She smudges out the grin and adds a 'sad' mouth.*
> *She turns to* RUTH.

BRONIA: What you doing with our sheets Ru?

RUTH: I want to make a cover for the gap in the wall.
Edek will bring us better sheets anyway, and we've got
to stop the draught somehow. (*To herself*) Trouble is
I haven't got a needle. I suppose I'll have to make one
from a splinter.

> BRONIA *is balancing a stick of charred wood on her*
> *fingers. Finally she drops it. She drags her feet over to*
> *where* RUTH *is sitting and drapes her arms around*
> RUTH'S *neck from behind.*

BRONIA: How long have we been living in this cellar
Ruth?

RUTH: Don't know love — but look, at least we're safe
here. The Nazis haven't got time to come searching
across this side of the city for three lost kids.

> *Pause.* BRONIA *moves away and sits on a box oppo-*
> *site* RUTH. *She bites her fingernails.*

RUTH (*a little sharp*): Don't do that Bron!
  BRONIA *starts to cry.*
RUTH (*exasperated*): Oh Bronia, pull yourself together:
  I only *spoke* to you.
BRONIA: Please, Ruth, I don't know what to *do*. I'm fed
  up with this place. I don't like the rats. I want Mummy
  and Daddy to come back!
RUTH (*crosses to her*): I'm sorry. I know it's not much
  fun for you. It's no joke for me either. Edek will be
  back soon. He's gone to the Polish Council to try to
  find out about Mum. (*She looks round rather hopelessly*)
  Why don't you do some more drawing?
BRONIA (*desperately*): There's no more wall left Ru!
  RUTH *sees this is true. She is moved by a surge of
  compassion for her little sister. She hugs* BRONIA *and
  swings her on to a box. She sits down next to her,
  confidentially.*
RUTH: I know what we'll do! We'll do what we always did.
  Starting tomorrow you are going to *school*!
BRONIA (*amazed*): *Where* Ruth?
RUTH: Here, in this very room. We'll have our own school.
  Your friends from the street can come. I'm old enough
  to be your teacher. It'll do you all good. They can bomb
  every building in Warsaw, but it won't stop children
  learning how to add up and take away. And if there are
  no reading books . . . well, we'll have to *tell* each other
  stories!
  *She begins to be carried away by her own ideas,
  pacing up and down the cellar.* BRONIA *just sits and
  stares, wide-eyed.*
RUTH: We'll have lessons in the morning only. Plenty of
  time for play in the afternoon. We'll start with a Bible
  story — I shall have to remember carefully. Then arith-
  metic or writing. Then a break. We can do games and
  P.E. on the open site when there's not a raid —
  EDEK *enters. She stops abruptly. There is a silence.*

EDEK (*forced cheerfulness*): I got some bread at the convent. (*Silence*) And I fixed up a job at the soup-kitchen: one of the boys was run in for theft . . . (*He breaks off*)

RUTH: Edek!

He can hide it no longer. He sits C. looking up at audience. RUTH *and* BRONIA *move to him.*

EDEK: They said Mum was taken to Germany to work on the land. But they can't say where.

Blackout 5 seconds.

Scene 3

JOSEPH (*narrator*): In the summer they left the city for the woods. Life was healthier there. They lived under an oak tree. When it rained, they got wet. When the sun shone it browned their limbs.

Because of the kindness of the peasants, food was more plentiful. It was forbidden to store food or to sell to anyone but the Nazis, but they gave the children whatever they could spare.

They hid it too, in cellars, in haystacks, in holes in the ground. With the help of the older children they smuggled it to the towns and sold it on the black market. Edek was a good smuggler. Ruth and Bronia were well fed, for he was well paid.

Improvisation VII: EDEK *barters with* PEASANT 2 *over barrow-load of filled logs which he is to take to the Peasant's accomplice in the market; ends with* EDEK *forcing price up.*

PEASANT 2: O.K. O.K. You're good. It's dangerous. Two rye loaves, apples and butter. Under the cattle trough in the top field tomorrow. Leave the cart in the first barn.

They shake hands on it. Exit PEASANT. EDEK *pushes away barrow to C., stops and turns to audience.*

EDEK: At school they taught me how to
Play the game
Follow the rules
'Honest' was my middle name

But now I know the two-faced world
More than I did before
Some rules are only for the rich
And others for the poor

To those who have, to them
Shall all the more be given
God bless the helpless
Their reward's in heaven!

Don't tell me that I'm cheating now
I know the score:
Trust yourself, trust no-one else:
Their game is war.

EDEK *pushes the barrow round in a circle. As he returns he meets a crowd — the market.* TWO GERMAN SOLDIERS *enter R.* EDEK *whistling, almost runs into them.*

SOLDIER 1: 'Ello what 'ave we 'ere then?
SOLDIER 2: Goin' somewhere, young man?
SOLDIER 1: Anythin' to declare?
SOLDIER 2: Anythin' we ought to know about?
SOLDIER 1: Got a pretty sister at 'ome?
SOLDIER 2: Get on wiv me mate would she?
SOLDIER 1: What's on yer wagon mate?
SOLDIER 2: Logs in summer?
SOLDIER 1: Suspicious!
SOLDIER 2: Most suspicious!
SOLDIER 1: 'Ave a look shall we?
SOLDIER 2: Wouldn't be tryin' t' pull a fast one eh?
SOLDIER 1: Stop us seein' the wood for the trees?
SOLDIERS *begin to examine the logs.* EDEK *is off,*

*like a rabbit. He dodges among the crowd who obstruct
the soldiers. He makes his escape up the audience steps
R. The* SOLDIERS *stop at the bottom.*

SOLDIER 1: 'E's got away!

SOLDIER 2: Yeh — I know 'im 'e's slippery as an eel. But
I got 'im marked down — we'll get 'im next time.

They disappear into shadow, audience R.

Scene 4

Cellar interior: RUTH *is standing before the 'class' of
ragged school children.*

RUTH: So although the king knew he had been tricked, he
had to go through with it. He called for Daniel and sent
him into the den. And he rolled a huge stone over the
entrance of the den and sealed it himself. Then he went
back to his palace, but he couldn't sleep, thinking about
Daniel, wondering if the lions would devour him.

Well, when morning came, he rushed out and rolled
back the stone and there stood Daniel, all in one piece,
with the lions dozing quietly around him. And Daniel
said: 'O King live forever, my God has sent an angel who
shut the lions' mouths and they have not hurt me'.

She stops, sighs, satisfied.

EVA (*after a pause*): Please Ruth — Miss — are you going
to tell us what the story means?

Others murmur 'Yes — you always tell us ... etc.

RUTH: Why don't you tell me, Eva? Your meaning is as
good as anyone else's.

EVA *looks down at her feet.*

RUTH (*smiles*): Don't worry, Eva. (*Pause*) Well, sometimes
I think of it as the story of our own troubles. The lions
are: cold and hunger and hardship. But if only we are
patient and trustful like Daniel, we will be delivered
from them ...

(*she falters*)

Sometimes though I see the lions scowling and snarling. . . . (*snapping out of it*), No! never mind that. We've been in this damp cellar too long this morning. Out you go everybody: into the sun!

Improvisation VIII: *The children play 'Air-raid alert'*
RUTH *remains in cellar C. While attention is focused on game* JAN *drags himself close to edge of stage — Audience L. and collapses unseen.*

BRONIA (*runs towards* JAN, *sees him, stops, approaches him cautiously. After a pause*): Ruth, Ruth, there's a boy lying down outside and he won't get up.

RUTH: Tickle his ribs!

BRONIA: I don't think he can get up.

RUTH: Who is it?

BRONIA: It's not one of the class. I've never seen him before.

    RUTH *goes to investigate.*

RUTH (*to the children who have gathered round*): Does anyone know who he is? (*They shake their heads.*)

RUTH: He looks ill and starved. Yankel, will you help me lift him down to the cellar? And Eva, please find something for him to drink, some milk if you can get it.

    They move him to C.

    JAN *calls for his pet:* 'Where's Jimpy?' *One of the children fetches a crate with the cockerel from* JAN's *point of entrance.* JAN *calls the name again.*

RUTH: That's a fine name, what's yours?

    EVA *returns with cup.*

RUTH: All right you others, I think this young man needs a rest. Off you go and play again. (*They do so reluctantly*). (*To* JAN) Look, Eva's brought some milk for you. Sit up and drink it. You'll feel better in a minute.

    JAN *sits up and drinks.* BRONIA *comes back, whispers to* RUTH.

BRONIA (*to others*): He still won't tell us his name!

KATE (*brings* JAN'S *box from Audience L.*): I found this in the street where he was lying. I think it must be his.

BRONIA (*snatching box*): It's heavy and it rattles. He must be rich! Ruth, may we undo the string?

RUTH (*with authority*): Give the box to him. Nobody shall touch it without asking him.

> JAN *takes the box and smiles. The children clamour to find out what's inside.*

JAN (*holding the box out of reach*): No-one sees into my treasure box. But since you gave it back to me I'll tell you my name. It's Jan.

RUTH (*holds out her hand*): I'm Ruth, this is my sister Bronia. These children are from the street. They go to our school. (JAN *looks puzzled*) We live here in the cellar. There used to be three of us, but my brother Edek went out smuggling one day and never came back.

> *She looks across to Audience Right where* EDEK *appears momentarily and is arrested by the TWO SOLDIERS who have been waiting in the shadows. They search him and discover food being smuggled inside his coat.*

RUTH: Perhaps you will help us find him again. Perhaps now you have come we shall be lucky.

> *Lights to half on stage. Spot upon JOSEPH, narrator.*

JOSEPH: For some days Jan was too ill to leave. What he needed was rest, warmth and good solid food. Ruth was a good nurse. The children left him alone, but they scrounged for him what they could for food. By the time Jan was better he didn't want to go.

Edek had gone; Jan had arrived. The Germans went; the Russians arrived. Several streets away there appeared a brand new hut — a Russian control post. . . .

Scene 5

The Russian control post: desk, two chairs and sign, is set up Down L. IVAN *is on sentry duty C.* LIEU-TENANT *is seated at desk.* RUTH *marches smartly up to him, but then stops, uncertain how to address him.*

IVAN: Don't stand there staring at me little girl.

RUTH: I'm not a little girl. I'll be sixteen next week. And I want to see your officer.

IVAN: The whole of Warsaw wants to see my officer. Run away and play!

RUTH: It's very important.

IVAN: Run away!

RUTH (*angry*): It's all right for you. You've got plenty to eat and drink and warm clothes too, and a bed to sleep in. Didn't you come here to set us free? You must let me see your officer.

IVAN (*grins*): Well, seeing it's your birthday next week, I might stretch a point. But I don't hold out much hope he'll see you. (*He goes inside and whispers with* LIEUTENANT.)

IVAN (*returning*): The lieutenant says come back the year after next.

RUTH *pushes past him to the desk where worried* LIEUTENANT *is typing.*

IVAN: Hey, you young hussy, come out!

LIEUTENANT: Leave her to me Ivan. (*To* RUTH) You're a determined young lady.

RUTH: I'm not a little girl, anyway.

LIEUTENANT: What is it you want?

RUTH: I want food and clothes and blankets, pencils and as much paper as you can spare. I've got sixteen children — (LIEUTENANT *gasps*) — seventeen if you count the one that's lost. He really is mine — he's my brother Edek. So is my sister Bronia. The others are just my school. They're all half starving and they're keen to learn and they've got nothing to write on. And I want you to help me find Edek. He's been lost over a year.

LIEUTENANT: Anything else you'd like me to do? (*He waves a thick pad of papers*) See this file? It's full of missing people, about ten to each page. All Warsaw's missing!

RUTH: One more name won't make a lot of difference then.

LIEUTENANT: I might as well burn the lot for all the good it is.

RUTH: Oh, don't do that. The writing's only on one side. Give me the papers and we can use the blank sides in school for writing on.

LIEUTENANT (*laughs*): O.K. Sit down. I'll take your particulars. But I warn you nothing will come of it.

He takes RUTH'S *name. She gives her address as* 'Bombed cellar, Liberation Street'. *Meanwhile* IVAN *returns with a pile of blankets and two bags: sugar and flour.*

IVAN: Er. 'Scuse me sir, but I was tidying up and found these lying around the sentries' billet. What d'you think I'd better do with them?

LIEUTENANT (*laughs again*): Well young lady, they say fortune helps those who help themselves. You'd better sign here for the blankets. The sugar and the flour won't be missed anyway.

RUTH signs and takes the pile from IVAN, *grinning. She runs back to the cellar.* IVAN *smiling shouts after her.*

IVAN: It's more than you deserve you little minx!

Spot on JOSEPH R. *Control post disappears, children set up birthday party in cellar C.*

JOSEPH (*narrator*):

> Sixteen years old
> Mother to as many children
> Your own uncertain youthfulness
> Stolen by war

Perhaps when you are twenty
It will be over, forgotten.
Perhaps then there will be time
To be a girl again.

Scene 6

Cellar interior: the birthday party. RUTH *is explaining how she made the cake.*

RUTH: So you see the soldier gave me flour and sugar and I made an oven out of a biscuit tin. Mind you I didn't think it would come out like this. Have you got the candles Bron?

BRONIA: What a pity there's only three. You'll be able to blow them out easily!

RUTH: Oh, I don't know Bron. Three's better than two, and two's better than one. (*She puts the candles in: suddenly grave*) One for me, one for you (*Pause*) and one for Edek.

IVAN approaches from L. JAN *leaps out of the shadow of the cellar at him, box in one hand, knife in the other. They roll.* IVAN *crushes the box.* JAN *ends up on top and flicks out the switchblade.*

RUTH (*rushing up to restrain him*): Jan, drop that knife at once! Drop it — d'you hear me?

Reluctantly JAN *obeys and closes the blade.*

IVAN (*rising to sit, dusting cap*): That's a pretty welcome I must say!

RUTH (*taking knife*): You must understand Jan, Ivan is our friend.

JAN: He's a soldier!

RUTH: A Russian soldier, not a Nazi! They've come to set us free and look after us.

JAN: I hate soldiers. They're all the same. I know them!

RUTH: I'm sorry about him, Ivan; his manners have been shaken up a bit recently. Come inside. We're about to start the party. You shall have the seat of honour.

They all go in except JAN *who picks up his broken box and sulks by the cellar wall.*

RUTH (*giving* IVAN *a box to sit on*): Head of the table!

IVAN (*jumps up rubbing his seat*): Two inches of rusty nail! That's not the sort of honour I appreciate. Did nobody ever teach you how to use a hammer?

RUTH: I haven't got a hammer. I used half a brick. (*She demonstrates, flattening the nail.* IVAN *sits.*)

IVAN: Brought a present for you. Nothing much. But my kids at home are fond of it. Bar of chocolate.

BRONIA: What's chocolate?

They crowd round for a piece each as RUTH *thanks him and divides it up.*

IVAN: Just about a crumb each. They won't get a taste from that. Wish I'd brought some more. But I came here for another reason. I've got news for you little gir— young lady. We've traced your brother. He's in a transit camp in Posen.

RUTH *jumps for joy and hugs* IVAN. BRONIA *joins in.*

IVAN (*embarrassed*): What would the wife say if she could see me now? Of course I had to handle the matter myself. If the lieutenant had done it, nothing would have come of it.

Here's the name and location of the camp. (*He fishes a slip of paper from his pocket.*) And something else that might come in handy. (*From his kit bag he takes a bundle of typewriting paper and pencils.*)

BRONIA (*clapping her hands, jumping*): I'll draw lots of pictures for you Ivan — fighting on the floor, sitting on the nail . . .

(*Pause*)

Did you pay for this all by yourself?

IVAN: That's not the way we do things in the army.

RUTH: I hope you didn't steal it.

IVAN: That's not the word we use for it. Just *re-allocated* it, you might say. It's a help for you and it's a help to the lieutenant because he can't wear himself out typing any more.

RUTH: Don't tell Jan. He's a dreadful thief, and it will only make him worse. (*She looks up to see* JAN *in the doorway. He is crying.*)

IVAN: Cheer up son. I've forgiven you, even if you did want to cut off my head for a souvenir.

JAN (*holding out his box*): You rolled on it. Thug!

IVAN: I'll mend it for you.

RUTH *tries to take the box: it falls in pieces with the sword to the floor.* RUTH *picks up the sword and holds it up to the light. The stage lights fade on* RUTH *last.*

ACT THREE

Scene 1

IVAN (*narrator*):

> When the snow melts, laughter runs in
> the streams.
> When the storks return after the winter,
> songs welcome them home.
>
> Father and daughter; sister and brother;
>
> Hear now the story of how the lost were
> brought together!

Spring was bursting when Ruth, Jan and Bronia left Warsaw on the first stage of their long journey to Switzerland. The road was crowded; many others were journeying too.

Enter L. RUTH *with blankets strapped to her back, food-bag and change of clothes under her arm.* JAN *with Jimpy and his new treasure box.* BRONIA *with her own small rucksack. They stop at the edge of the stage. The* REFUGEES *are moving slowly but purposefully across the stage, singly and in twos or threes in both directions. It is a kind of crossroads.*

RUTH: Well, goodbye to Warsaw! Which is the road to Posen do you think?

BRONIA: Will we find Edek when we get to Posen?

RUTH: That's where Ivan said they'd traced him. But it's a long way and three of us and a bird aren't going to get many lifts. It's a long way to walk, Bron.

BRONIA: I don't mind walking. It'll be easy with my new shoes. I'm sorry we missed Ivan though. I wanted to thank him. Shoes are the best present anyone could have!

JAN: My new box is better! Anyway we need to get a lift. Jimpy's tired of being carried and we can't walk fifty miles. The road's just rubble.

RUTH: Look Jan, we're going to Posen, we're going to find Edek and we're going on to Switzerland. That's where you said our father was going, right?

JAN: Yes. He said so when he gave me the sword. I don't remember anything else: except the determination on his face.

RUTH: That's Dad alright, but you're ready to give up before we've started. You must make your choice now. Go back to the cellar — you can stay with the children — or come with us and no complaining.

JAN (*decisively*): I'm coming with you!

A family group passes, tugging a cart piled up with furniture. RUTH *steps forward.*

RUTH: Excuse me! Which is the way to Posen?

REFUGEE WIFE: Follow us.

They join the crowd which continues to move to and fro. They begin in a 'round' to sing.

> When the bombs fall; pack up your bags.
> Grin and start walking, don't look sad.
> If your house is razed to the ground
> Stifle the groan and smother the frown.
> Somewhere, someone's worse off than you.
> Home is where you're travelling to.

IVAN (*narrator*): After four days on the road they reached Posen. Bronia's feet were blistered, Jan was tired, Jimpy was dazed with the jogging. This city was not as flat as Warsaw. Some buildings were still standing.

TWO RUSSIAN SOLDIERS *set up a control post C. at which the* REFUGEES *stop and are directed or turned*

back. RUTH *produces the slip of paper which the* 1ST
RUSSIAN SOLDIER *looks at. Passes to* 2ND SOLDIER.

2ND SOLDIER: You want the Old Kolinsky Barracks,
Miss. It's about a mile that-a-way. Big building, by the
river. You can't mistake it: crumbling front — miserable
looking place.

The children cross the stage to R. where a SECRE-
TARY *sits at a desk.*

SECRETARY (*looks up*): Sorry! No children!

RUTH (*ushers the others back and goes over to the desk —
very polite*): I'm sorry to trouble you but we're looking
for my brother Edek Balicki. We were told he was
resting here.

SECRETARY: Wait a minute. (*She goes 'inside'.* RUTH
turns to others and raises eyebrows. SECRETARY
returns, looking over her glasses) Baliski, did you say?

RUTH: Balicki.

SECRETARY (*thumbs through a file*): We've only just
taken over here: the records are in a complete mess.
Typical! (*Pause*) I'll check again. (*Pause*) Balicki . . .
No, sorry Miss, no Balicki on our records.

RUTH: He must be here. When I heard he was here I
wrote to you to say we were coming.

SECRETARY: There's no postal service.

RUTH: I sent it through the military.

SECRETARY (*looks back at her and shakes her head*):
Sorry.

RUTH: Look, he's tall, brown hair. . . .

She goes on describing him when a DOCTOR *passing,
steps across to them.*

DOCTOR: Did you say Edek Balicki?

RUTH (*excited*): Yes, he's my brother!

DOCTOR: I sent him yesterday to the Warthe camp with
the other TB cases.

RUTH: But . . . Was he . . . Please wait a minute! (*But he
is gone.*)

SECRETARY: The camp's only a mile down the river. Won't you stay and have something to eat first? You look dreadfully tired and hungry.

RUTH: Yes. . . . I am. We all are. If Edek is ill we must go straight away. Look, my friend and my sister are outside; I must go.

RUTH (*goes to the others*): Come on. It's getting dark; We've got to find a place called the Warthe Camp.

The children cross again to L. An ORDERLY *stands in the spot.*

RUTH: Is this the Warthe camp?

ORDERLY: Yes, Miss.

RUTH: I believe my brother may be here.

ORDERLY: One moment Miss.

He steps back into the darkness and returns with the REGISTRAR.

REGISTRAR (*looks them up and down*): Are you Edek Balicki's family?

RUTH: Yes, Sir.

REGISTRAR: I saw quite a lot of him. (*Pause*) But I'm sorry to say he is no longer here. He was a wild boy. He ran away this morning. I can't tell you where. We had no time to run after him. There are so many here who need our help. We cannot waste time on those who refuse it. (*The children turn away to C. exhausted and depressed.*) Er. . . . I gather there's a field kitchen just set up in Kolina. Red Cross place. You might at least get a square meal there. . . .

Scene 2

The three children are standing dejectedly when they are overtaken by a jabbering group of REFUGEES *who come from stage R. and almost sweep the three to L. where a second group press them back toward centre. The Field Kitchen is set up R. and* RELIEF OFFICER *steps forward, hands raised to prevent the babbling crowd from swamping it.*

RELIEF OFFICER: Listen! Listen! (*They keep on jabbering*) Please! (*exasperated*) There will be no food until I have an orderly queue! (*Instant silence*) Right! Those who have had one meal since they arrived sit down there please! New arrivals and children under twelve queue there. (*Some of the crowd sit, most form a queue diagonally R. to up C.*) We call this meal dinner, though I don't suppose that matters to most of you.

The queue is silent, the COOK *tries to cheer them up.*

COOK: Right then, me darlings: first course, soup of the day. This'll put a bit of warmth in you! (*They file along taking a bowl, a ladle of soup is slopped in, and a hunk of bread.*) Don't look so miserable, the war's over, I tell you. The Russian armies have met the Americans on the Elbe. Germany's done for! (*Pause, the children are intent on their soup.*)

ASSISTANT: Wonderful news isn't it? I don't know what's wrong with these children. You'd think it would cheer them up to hear the war's over, but they don't seem to hear you.

COOK (*to* JAN, *as he arrives holding a bowl*): You sonny — you with the eagle in the basket — aren't you glad the bombs have stopped dropping? (JAN *does not respond.*) Cockerel is it? Don't look very happy either. Better 'ave an extra dollop to make him sit up and crow. (*As* JAN *is turning away*) I'll 'ave 'im for soup if 'e's no good to you!

JAN *turns back as if to strike the* COOK, *but as he turns he loses his bowl and bread which fall in front of the rest of the queue. All the children and those on the ground pile in after the pieces.*

RELIEF OFFICER: Hey. Stop it! Little animals. There's plenty . . . (*he sees it's useless.*)

As the scrum is uncovered we see RUTH *at the bottom, clutching a hand. It is* EDEK'S.

EDEK (*sitting up*): Well, fancy meeting you at a place like this.

>   RUTH *cries.* BRONIA *bounces with happiness.*
> JAN *looks dazed.*

RUTH (*through her sobbing*): We thought you were in Germany. Then we thought we were going to find you. Then you were gone again. Oh Edek! (*More tears: she grasps his two hands.*)

RELIEF OFFICER (*rather embarrassed*): Now come on you two. I don't know what this is all about but you're holding up the proceedings.

>   *The three children are ushered forward to spot C.*
> *The remaining stage lights fade imperceptibly to end of*
> *scene.* RELIEF OFFICER *hands them bowls of soup*
> *and bread.* JAN *is standing behind* RUTH *to R. of spot.*
> *As* EDEK *tells his story the others gather round to listen,*
> *one by one.*

EDEK: I was caught smuggling cheese into Warsaw, and they sent me back to Germany to slave on the land. The farm was near Guben and the slaves came from all parts of Europe, women mostly and boys of my age. In winter we cut peat to manure the soil. We were at it all day from dawn to dusk. In spring we did sowing — cabbage crop mostly. At harvest time we packed the cabbage heads in crates and sent them into town. We lived on the outer leaves — they tasted bitter. I tried to run away but they always fetched me back. Last winter, when the war turned against the Nazis and the muddles began, I succeeded. I hid under a train, under a cattle wagon, and lay on top of the axle with my arms and legs stretched out.

JAN: When the train started, you fell off.

EDEK: Afterwards I sometimes wished I had, that is, until I found Ruth and Bronia again. Somehow I managed to cling on and I got a free ride back to Poland.

JAN: Liar! You're making it all up. There's no room to lie under a truck. Nothing to hold on to.

EDEK (*stands and squares up to him*): Have you ever
looked under a truck? Every axle is braced by a pair of
struts, about this far apart (*stretches arms*). I just lay
on the axle-bar and clung on above my head.

JAN: Get away! You haven't the strength. . . .

They are about to come to blows as the RELIEF
OFFICER *steps in and pushes them apart.*

JAN (*sitting*): You would have been shaken off like a
rotten plum!

EDEK: That's what anyone would expect, but if you shut
up and listen, I'll tell you why I wasn't. (*Pause*) Lying
on my stomach I found the view rather monotonous.
It made me dizzy too. I had to shut my eyes. And the
bumping! Then the train ran through a puddle, no more
than a puddle — it must have been a flood, for I was
splashed and soaked right through. But that water saved
me. After that I couldn't let go, even if I'd wanted to.

JAN: Why not?

EDEK: The water froze on me. It made an icicle of me.
When at last the train drew into a station, I was encased
in ice from head to foot. I could hear Polish voices on
the platform. I knew we must have crossed the frontier.
My voice was the only part of me that wasn't frozen, so
I shouted. The station master came and chopped me
down with an axe. He wrapped me in blankets and
carried me to the boiler-house to thaw out. Took me
hours to thaw out.

2ND REFUGEE WIFE: You don't look properly thawed
out yet.

2ND REFUGEE: Give him a blanket.

3RD REFUGEE: A tall story, but he's earned a bed by the
stove.

4TH REFUGEE: Another story, somebody!

*The lights which have closed on the circle fade during
this speech.*

5TH REFUGEE: How about a story for the children?

Something fantastic — no soldiers, no bombs — prin-
cesses and dragons. Lek — you tell the story of Krakus'
daughter. Bridgit get your guitar, we'll have music and a
fire after dinner. . . .

IVAN (*narrator*): It would have been easy to stay in Kolina.
Edek was not well. The doctors wanted him to return to
the hospital. Only the welfare officer knew how much
their journey meant to them.

    MRS BOROWICZ — *the welfare officer* — *joins him
in his spot.*

MRS BOROWICZ: Those children insist on going on to
Switzerland — it's their promised land — and we've no
power to detain them. Edek is sick, but he believes his
father's at the other end, waiting. Highly unlikely, of
course, but there's a sort of fierce resolution about the
boy — about all of them — which saves them from
despair, and it's better than any medicine we can give
them. Dope and drugs can't equal that. We must let
them go. (*Exit*)

Scene 3

    Half-a-dozen bales upstage C. A signal gantry L.

IVAN (*narrator*): Poland to Switzerland; in the atlas at
school it was not far. On the road, an inch is a thousand
miles. Progress was slow; sometimes they fell into despair.

    Sometimes there was a train — food — another city —
Potsdam — Berlin. By June they had reached the American Zone.

    Lights up: enter the three children and JAN — *worn,*
EDEK *coughing. He leans on* JAN'S *shoulder to get his
breath.*

RUTH: It's no good. We've reached the limit. We'll have to
rest. Bron, take Edek's bag and sit down in the shade.
(*She draws* JAN *aside — to* JAN *only*) He won't stop
unless we make him. But if we go on like this he won't

ever see father. Last night he coughed all night. I don't think he slept a wink. If we can convince Edek he needs a new pair of shoes — anything — we might be able to keep him in one place long enough to let him get his strength back. (*Going over to the others*) Jan and I have a plan. We need some money, for food, new clothes — shoes — so we're going to try for work. Jan can go hay-making. I'll have to get some cleaning job — I'll try the local school or the government offices. Bronia, your job will be to look after Edek while we're away. We can set up camp in one of the meadows. A week or two off the road will do us all no end of good.

IVAN (*narrator*): They found a pleasant site in a meadow by a mill stream. At night they kept a fire; a chill wind blew, even in summer. For a roof they had a willow tree, for light, the stars.

So Edek rested well — and ate well too, for there was no shortage of food. Several times Jan came home from work with a bag full of such food as they had never tasted before — chicken, lobster, salted pork and luncheon meat.

RUTH (*draws* EDEK *downstage*): I know he's stealing it. It's American food. When I ask him where he gets it he says it's from the farmer.

EDEK: No-one's that generous in wartime. I think he's getting it from the depot.

RUTH: I don't know — the depot is closely guarded and I've never seen him anywhere near. If he's thieving he'll get caught. The Americans don't miss much. There's a hall next to the school and a military court trying cases all day long.

EDEK: He brought back nothing yesterday, or the day before. Perhaps his source has dried up.

RUTH: He says the farmer promised him more tomorrow.

EDEK: I'll get to the bottom of it. I'll watch him when he leaves work tomorrow. Just don't let on. . . .

RUTH *and* BRONIA *exit.* EDEK *hides audience R.* JAN *is half hidden behind the bales C. Suddenly a ragged boy sprints from L. to C. keeping low. There is a moment's whispering before the boy sprints away R. and* JAN *disappears behind the bales. Long pause.* JAN *appears just as suddenly and runs to gantry, climbs and lies down flat upon it. Begins to work with wire cutters and spanner.*

EDEK (*crossing in concern*): What's the game Jan? You're not a train wrecker!

JAN *swears at him — suddenly the signal falls.*

JAN: Go away, you fool, go away!

Sound of approaching train.

EDEK: You'll cause an accident!

JAN: Idiot! Go away!

He escapes down one side as EDEK *climbs gantry on the other side, gasping and coughing.* EDEK *totters to his feet and waves frantically, back to audience. Sound of train stopping. Whistle.* U.S. MILITARY POLICE-MAN *appears from R. pointing a pistol.*

POLICEMAN: O.K. You, come down slowly. No tricks. When you get to the ground turn round and face me!

Blackout 5 seconds

Scene 4

As the lights come up CAPTAIN GREENWOOD *is seated behind a table R. stacking a sheaf of papers. The Prosecutor,* JAMES *is standing to the left. He too has a file of notes.*

GREENWOOD (*sighs*): What's the next case, James? I think we've got time for one more before lunch.

JAMES: It's an odd one, Captain. Edek Balicki, fourteen, a Pole — no address — caught interfering with signals. He's one of a gang we've been watching for some time. They do a very clever line in stopping trains.

GREENWOOD: O.K. (*calls*) Next! (*A* G.I. *ushers* EDEK *in*) Are you Edek Balicki?

EDEK: Yes.

GREENWOOD (*mechanically*): You are charged with stopping a railway train with intent to steal U.S. Government property on June twentieth this year. Do you plead guilty or not guilty?

EDEK: I did stop the train, but I didn't steal anything. And I didn't *intend to steal* anything.

GREENWOOD: There's a gang who've been robbing trains in this area for a month. We realise you're probably not the organiser — just in it for once, for a game maybe — so if you tell us all you know you're more likely to get off lightly.

EDEK: I don't know anything about a gang; I just stopped that one train.

JAMES: Come on, you can't expect us to believe that. People don't just stop trains for no reason. (EDEK *is silent.*)

GREENWOOD: Well, why did you stop the train, Edek?

EDEK (*after a pause*): It was a prank. I wanted to see if it really would stop.

JAMES: You don't look like the kind of boy who delights in 'pranks' of that sort.

EDEK *shrugs.*

GREENWOOD: Young man, it's my job to be fair. But I represent the American government. We can't help you people if you're not prepared to co-operate with us. I warn you, I intend to get to the bottom of this, sooner or later. Do you have anyone to defend you? Lieutenant James is an experienced Military Prosecutor. It's his job to present the Authority's case against you.

EDEK: I don't want anyone defending me. There's nothing to defend.

GREENWOOD: Very well. There will be no attempt to

bully you, but you can't expect soft treatment from James. (*To* JAMES) Carry on.

JAMES: These tools, (*he produces the wire cutters* JAN *used and the hammer*) where did you get them?

EDEK: They're not mine.

JAMES: Do you mean that we shouldn't believe that you used them to alter the signal? They were found where you were standing. . . .

Enter G.I. CORPORAL, *standing to attention.*

CORPORAL: Permission to speak to Captain Greenwood, sir!

GREENWOOD *nods,* CORPORAL *steps forward and whispers to him.*

GREENWOOD: Sure — if they can help us. Show them in.

RUTH, JAN *and* BRONIA *are shown in and made to stand beside* EDEK.

RUTH: There's been a mistake and I've come to explain. This is Jan. It's all his fault. I want to speak for him.

GREENWOOD: Who is the other child?

RUTH: My sister Bronia. She has nothing to do with this, but I had to bring her along as I've nowhere to leave her. We're on our way to Switzerland and are camping by the mill-stream.

GREENWOOD: I see. What's the boy's full name?

RUTH: Only Jan — that's the only name we know.

GREENWOOD: Jan, have you any parents?

JAN: The grey cat and Jimpy, but they're dead, and Ruth's my mother now.

RUTH: I think he's an orphan. We found him half dead on a bomb-site in Warsaw. I've been a kind of mother to him since then. He won't talk about his past. All he tells us is that he wants to stay with us. In a way he looks after us. And in a way we look after him.

GREENWOOD: We take it then that you have no parents, but that this young lady, Ruth Balicki, is your guardian. You claim that Edek Balicki is wrongly accused.

42

Lieutenant James here will read the charge again. Listen carefully, Jan, and then answer our questions.

JAMES *repeats the charge directly to* JAN.

GREENWOOD: Guilty or not guilty?

JAN *makes a bolt for the door.* CORPORAL *and* G.I. *bring him back, kicking and biting.*

GREENWOOD: Stop that kicking! (*To* RUTH) Have you any control over the boy?

RUTH: He's scared of soldiers. If you'd kindly send those guards outside, sir, I think he'd behave himself.

GREENWOOD: Release the prisoner and wait outside the door.

They release JAN *and exit.* JAN *is left panting and angry on the floor.*

GREENWOOD: Stand up. (JAN *does so.*) We are here to know the truth. Now Jan, will you tell us in your own words what happened?

JAN (*looking round suspiciously*): I don't have to.

RUTH: No more hanky-panky, Jan. Or you know what you'll get!

JAN (*with eyes lowered*): It's not Edek's fault. I changed the signal and he came to stop me. I ran away and he was caught. He needn't have been caught, but he's a very stupid boy for his age. He makes a mess of everything.

GREENWOOD: What made you want to stop the train?

JAN: The food trucks.

GREENWOOD: You were going to raid them yourself?

JAN: No.

GREENWOOD: You were one of a gang?

JAN: Yes.

GREENWOOD: Was Edek Balicki a member?

JAN: No. He had nothing to do with the business.

GREENWOOD: Who are the others?

JAN: You mean the train robbers? I never met any of them and I don't know anything about them. If I did,

43

I wouldn't tell. Those soldiers can go and sniff them out.

RUTH (*producing a stick from behind her back, clouts* JAN'S *rear*): That's for being rude.

JAN *apologises, murmuring sheepishly.*

GREENWOOD: Lieutenant James, do you wish to cross-examine the witness?

JAMES (*flourishing his papers with some importance*): I do indeed. (*Clears his throat and leans towards* JAN) What did this gang pay you for your services?

JAN: Nothing.

JAMES: You ask me to believe that you undertook this dangerous task for nothing?

JAN: Of course. There was nothing to give me. The train wasn't robbed. But the other times ... (JAN *stops short, bites his lip.*)

JAMES: Would you explain what you mean by 'the other times'?

JAN: They gave me a share of the food they took. And jolly good stuff it was.

BRONIA (*shouts out*): Except for that fat ham, that made us all sick ... OW! (*She cries out as* RUTH *raps her knuckles.*)

JAMES (*ignoring interruption*): I see. They gave you some of the loot. But you said just now that you never met any of them. How could they give you food without your seeing them?

JAN (*smiling*): They're a lot smarter than you think, Lieutenant. They left it for me in a hiding place in the wood.

JAMES: How many times did this happen?

JAN: Twice.

GREENWOOD: You are going beyond the terms of the charge, Lieutenant James. Nothing will be gained by pursuing this line any further now.

JAMES: With respect, sir, I ...

GREENWOOD (*interrupts*): Are you satisfied that the prisoner is guilty of the charge you have brought?

JAMES: Perfectly.

GREENWOOD: Then we can leave the matter at that. Have you no further relevant questions to put?

JAMES (*barks with a little annoyance*): No sir. (*Bangs his papers on the desk and sits down*)

GREENWOOD (*turns to* JAN *and speaks gently*): Why did you go in for stealing when you can get plenty to eat at the food kitchens?

JAN (*bitterly*): We can't live otherwise.

GREENWOOD: It has become a general habit, a bad habit.

JAN: The Nazis stole everything from our country and left us with nothing; now it is our turn to steal from them.

GREENWOOD: But this is American food you have been stealing, not Nazi food. It is sent here to feed you and all the other refugees that are flooding the country. If you steal it you are robbing your own people. Do you think that is right or sensible?

JAN: I want to feed Ruth and Bronia and Edek. (*Tears begin to roll down his cheeks.*) Edek is ill and we are all hungry. I shall always steal if they are hungry.

GREENWOOD: Do they steal?

JAN: No. They are not as clever as I am. But everybody else does, even the Americans. They take cameras and glasses from the Germans. There's a hundred cases of wine in your canteen, all stolen. I know where they got it from.

GREENWOOD: Those are not proper observations. (*Stands*) It will not help your case to bandy wild accusations of that sort. If there's any truth in them, they'll be brought to my notice and dealt with in the correct way.

RUTH *slips an arm round* JAN'S *shoulder in comfort, whispers in his ear.*

JAN (*realises* RUTH *wants him to apologise, swallows hard*): I speak with respect, sir.

GREENWOOD (*smiles*): When I was your age, Jan, I was brought up on the ten commandments. Maybe they're out of fashion now. One of them is 'Thou shalt not steal' — ever heard of it?

JAN: It doesn't work.

GREENWOOD: It must be made to work, or everything will go to pieces. Don't forget that. (*Shuffles the papers on his desk, then passes sentence*) Edek Balicki not guilty, case dismissed. Jan has pleaded guilty. Under the circumstances I shall deal with him as lightly as I can. 200 marks fine or 7 days.

    RUTH *and* JAN *consult each other.*

RUTH: Jan says he'll take the detention. We haven't enough money to pay the fine.

BRONIA: We're saving up to buy a pair of boots for Edek.

RUTH: Thank you, sir.

GREENWOOD: It isn't long, Jan, and you'll be looked after. When you come out, stick to that mother, as she's old enough not to have forgotten what decent behaviour is. (*Smiles*) Remind her to send me a postcard when you get to Switzerland!

    RUTH *holds* JAN'S *hand tightly till the guards come for him. He goes without a struggle, not daring to look back at her.*

    When he has gone, RUTH *gives one hand to* EDEK *and one to* BRONIA *and they walk slowly out.*

Scene 5

IVAN (*narrator*): So there was a pause on the journey. When Jan was released, they took to the road again. As the children trudged the steep Bavarian roads the days grew shorter. At night they sought the shelter of the warm hay-barns.

    Lights rise on a pile of bales — dim interior. Enter R the FARMER *with a pitchfork.*

FARMER: Alright you little devil. Come out of there!
I can hear you snoring.

Long silence. Then BRONIA *sobs, muffled.*

FARMER: Come out! Or I'll smoke you out like rabbits.
(*Pause*) Or poke you out with my fork!

*Silence. Then a turnip flies out from the bales, aimed
at the* FARMER.

That does it! (*He wades in with the handle of the pitch-
fork.*)

RUTH'S VOICE: We give in! Please put that horrible thing
away before it goes right through Bronia!

One by one, RUTH, BRONIA *and* EDEK *emerge,
straw in their clothes and hair.*

EDEK: We only spent the night here. We haven't done any
harm.

From this point, the FARMER *is more kindly, mildly
amused. He speaks in a warm accent: a countryman but
no yokel.*

FARMER: No harm! (*Picking up turnip*) I suppose you
call this a birthday present! One, two, three of you. Is
that the lot, or are there more of you lurking somewhere?

JAN *lobs a second turnip before emerging.* BRONIA
giggles.

JAN: Run out of ammo!

RUTH: When will you grow up, you silly little boy! (*She
seizes him by the shoulders and shakes him like a
puppy.*) You spoil everything for us. I wish we'd left
you in Warsaw.

JAN: Don't go for me, Ruth. I haven't stolen anything.
The larder window was open all night and I could have
taken anything I wanted, but I didn't — you know I
didn't!

RUTH: You'd better get on your knees and apologise.

JAN *remains standing but mumbles an apology.*

FARMER: Fair enough! I don't think there's any lasting
bomb damage. (*To* EDEK) Now, Mr Spokesman, maybe

you'll be kind enough to explain what you're doing here.

EDEK: Well, sir, we're travelling south, to Lake Constance. We want to cross into Switzerland: our father is there. He was a schoolmaster in Warsaw. We got split up when the fighting swept through. We got here after dark. We usually ask permission, but last night there were no lights on and we didn't like to disturb the household. We'll willingly pay for our night's lodging with a day's work.

FARMER: Dead right you will. And if I'm not satisfied with you, I could always hand you over to the Burgomeister.

BRONIA: What's a bergermaster?

FARMER: Don't know what it is where you come from, but around here it's a nasty, nosey, official individual that pesters folk beyond endurance. He'd be particularly interested in refugees like you. I've had Polish kids sleeping in this barn before now — working for us too. But now there's an order out from the Military Government that all foreigners found hereabouts should be rounded up and sent back where they came from.

RUTH		We haven't come eight-hundred miles just to be shipped back again!
BRONIA		We're going to find our father and
	(together):	mother. No-one's going to stop us!
EDEK		Nothing on earth would persuade me to go back now.
JAN		Nor me!

FARMER: Well you may say. But the law is the law, and rotten turnips'll do no good if the Burgomeister and the Military come round after you. (*Pause*) But I'm in no hurry to tell him you're here, and I don't reckon the soldiers'll be out of their beds yet. You've got time for a bite of breakfast before I set you to work.

Lights quick fade. Hold 5 seconds. Up — bright exterior.

Improvisation IX: *Under the eye of the* FARMER, *the* CHILDREN *work in the fields with the* FARM LA-BOURERS — *a co-ordinated mime. As they work all chant, hum or sing a 'Bavarian' tune. The bales may be removed from the stage as part of the action. As the workers break from their toil, an impromptu peasant dance. Finally a parting: the* CHILDREN *take their leave of the* FARMER *upstage, warm handshakes, perhaps he gives* RUTH *a few coins, perhaps* BRONIA *gives him a hug. Meanwhile the* LABOURERS *gather their own belongings — implements and bundles. One or two pick up the children's bags for them. Sad farewells and waving as the* CHILDREN *walk slowly towards downstage R.* LABOURERS *exit L and R. Lights fade on all but* NARRATOR *and the children who are now in downstage spot R.*

Scene 6

IVAN (*narrator*): The children pressed on south to Falkenburg. They crossed the Danube. There was a lorry lift for some miles along the road to Switzerland. But after that, more walking. There were fewer places to shelter on the road. Three days later, tired but not dispirited, they camped by the roadside.

   RUTH *and* BRONIA *begin to spread blankets from the rucksack.* JAN *helps* EDEK.

RUTH: Only eighty more miles to Lake Constance!

BRONIA (*sleepy*): Is Lake Constance in Switzerland?

RUTH: Switzerland is on the far shore of the lake. Lie down here, Bronia. The grass is nice and thick.

BRONIA: Will Mother be waiting for us on the shore?

RUTH (*with a lump in her throat*): Perhaps, Bron. Perhaps she will.

   A pause. The children settle down in their blankets. JAN *gets out his treasure-box and counts through the*

49

contents. *Suddenly he leaps to his feet.*

JAN: The sword's missing. Somebody's stolen it!

RUTH: Nobody would do that. Let me have a look! (*She searches in the box.*) When did you have it last? (JAN *shrugs.*) You showed it to Mr and Mrs Wolff at the farm, and you put it on the mantelpiece. Did you leave it there?

JAN (*horrorstruck*): Yes. (*He is motionless for a moment, then*) I've got to go back and get it!

He runs off toward L but RUTH *is too quick and drags him down to sit on his blanket.*

RUTH: Silly little idiot. The Wolffs are honest enough. They'll look after the sword until we send for it. I tell you what — you can busy yourself getting some kindling. We'll need a fire before morning.

EDEK *coughs.*

RUTH (*turning to* EDEK): You'd better have that jumper Mrs Wolff gave me. It's in the rucksack. (*She gets it for him.*)

EDEK (*wincing*): The pain in my chest is getting worse.

JAN *stops looking sullen and gets up and sets off L.*

JAN (*mutters*): I'm going to get the sword all the same.

EDEK: Where's he going?

JAN (*turning*): Only to get firewood! (*Exit*)

The spots begin a slow fade — dusk to darkness.

EDEK: I'll never be able to sleep. It's like a vice on my chest. You'd better go on without me tomorrow.

RUTH: You'll feel better in the morning.

EDEK: Can't walk any more.

RUTH: We'll get a lift. It's only eighty miles.

EDEK: There's no traffic going that way. (*Another bout of coughing. Long pause as they try to sleep.*)

JAN *creeps back. Lays down a bundle of sticks just on the spot edge. He crosses to* RUTH.

JAN (*stage whisper*): Ruth, may I have Edek's shoes when he dies?

RUTH (*forcing calm*): He's not going to die, Jan.

Pause.

JAN: He will if I don't have my sword. And we'll never find your father either. He gave me the sword and it's our lifeline. We can't do without it.

    EDEK *coughs.*

RUTH: Go to sleep, Jan. Everything will be all right.

    The slow fade has reached black. Very quietly in the darkness the tune of the peasant dance is hummed, fitfully, here and there backstage, in a minor transposition.

Scene 7

    The lights rise very slowly — dawn effect — the spot R first and gradually the whole stage from R to L. The stage exactly as before but JAN has disappeared.

    RUTH *wakes. Starts when she sees the empty blanket. She almost goes after JAN but turns to the others, sadly. She touches EDEK'S hand, then his cheek. She listens for his breathing. Reassured, she turns to the rucksack to get out breakfast.* BRONIA *stirs.*

BRONIA (*sitting up*): Where's Jan?

RUTH (*clipped*): He's gone off.

BRONIA (*cheerfully*): Well, Jan can look after himself.

RUTH: He forgets that we may need him to look after us.

    EDEK *rolls over and groans.*

BRONIA: Is he still asleep?

RUTH: Sort of. I don't think he'll be able to get up today let alone walk.

BRONIA: What's wrong with Edek? His eyes were all glassy yesterday.

RUTH: I expect it's just tiredness.

BRONIA: Yes.

    EDEK *rolls back and coughs.*

RUTH (*with sudden despair in her voice*): I don't know what it is, Bron, but he's in a bad way. We need help. We'd better get up to the road.

RUTH *and* BRONIA *roll their blankets and pack the rucksack in silence.* RUTH *rolls* EDEK'S *blanket while* BRONIA *tries to wake him up fully. Eventually, they lift him up and stagger a few paces towards downstage C.* EDEK *looks as if he is sleep-walking.*

BRONIA: Will we get a lift today?

RUTH: Of course we shall.

BRONIA: The driver yesterday said there's no traffic on this road going to Switzerland.

Pause.

RUTH: He was wrong. Look, isn't that something coming now?

Longer pause. BRONIA *steps forward and peers.*

BRONIA: Huh. It's only a man on a bike.

After a second or two he crosses: downstage L to upstage R. He stares at them but says nothing.

Long pause.

RUTH: I suppose I should have asked him for help. Never mind.

EDEK *mutters deliriously. They struggle to get out a canteen to give him a drink.* RUTH *opens the cap. Turns it upside down. Empty*

Another long pause. The children are looking towards L. Enter R, behind, WOMAN WITH BARROW. *She is scavenging for firewood. She sees Jan's sticks and makes a dart for them. The children turn.*

WOMAN: These yorn?

RUTH: Yes. But you can have them. (WOMAN *grabs them into her barrow.*) Er . . . My brother's sick. We need to get him to a doctor . . . to a village . . . can you . . .

WOMAN: Wos 'e got?

RUTH: I think it might be T.B.

The WOMAN *takes a step back and makes off backwards in a wide circle to upstage L exit.*

Long pause. Then sound of lorry from L. Distant, getting closer, stops.

BRONIA (*bouncing*): It's a truck. (*Sudden horror*) It's a military truck. Hadn't we better hide?

RUTH: No, Bron, stay here. We'll have to give ourselves up. Edek's so bad. It doesn't matter which way they take us.
   Sound of door. JOE *ambles in, chewing, from downstage L.*

JOE: Well, howdy. You in some kinda difficulty, Miss?

RUTH: Oh please, please, my brother's ill, we need a lift; we're going south. Can you help us?

JOE: Surely can. (*Taking a look at* EDEK) Now what exactly seems to be the trouble?

RUTH: He's in a state of collapse: we've been on the road for over a year. We've walked most of the way from Warsaw.

JOE (*surprised*): Say, are you Polish? My Ma an' Pa came out from Poland. I should 'a known that accent. It's good to hear a Polish voice again. (*Offering his hand*) Joe Wolski's the name — just call me Joe. You headed south you say.

RUTH: Yes, we're aiming for the Lake. Our parents are in Switzerland. (*Slight pause*) At least, we hope they are.

JOE: Gee, you've certainly come some way. I guess Warsaw's changed since I was there. I was only six when Ma and Pa took me to the States to settle. Lookin' back I don't recall that much, but it seems like they made the right move.

BRONIA: They did. Most of our part of the city's as flat as a pancake.

JOE: Here, take a hit on this, kid. (*He gives* EDEK *a drink from a small flask*) Best medicine I know! (*He offers the flask to* RUTH *who shakes her head*) Better get this wounded trooper up on the truck. There's a Red Cross Camp at Überlingen; that's just a stone's throw from the Lake. We can be there inside a coupla hours.

RUTH: That soon?

JOE: Way I drive, maybe sooner. (*To* BRONIA) You can

53

take a look at my wild animal collection when we get
there. Got'm all tied up in the back of the truck!

BRONIA (*puzzled*): What sort of animals, Joe?

JOE (*casually*): Oh, coupla bears an' a hyena.

BRONIA: Jan would have loved that!

JOE: Who's Jan, your boyfriend? (BRONIA *giggles*)

BRONIA: Actually, he's just an ordinary friend. He came
with us from Warsaw. But now he's run away. He'd lost
his sword. It's not a real sword, only a paper-knife. I
think he's gone back to get it. But if it's where we think
it is it's miles away.

JOE (*smiles and shakes his head*): Well, they say it's a
small world. You're certainly going to be interested in
my metaphorical menagerie!

BRONIA: What's a metaphorical, Ruth? (RUTH *just
smiles.*)

JOE (*to* BRONIA): I once knew a kid like Jan — a runaway.
Went to sleep in the back of my truck one night — alone,
mark you — and when I woke up in the morning, there
he was, stretched out beside me. Must have climbed in
over the tail-board during the night. I shook him awake
and asked what he was doing. Said he was going north,
and if I was going that way would I take him to — I
forget the name of the village. Some place north of the
Danube. Now I *was* going north as it happened, but
when I heard his business I changed my mind. I told him
he ought to have known better than to desert his folks.
He kicked and stormed at me as if he was crazy and
called me all the names that aren't in the dictionary.
Know what to do with a fella like that? You truss him
up and leave him to cool off in the back of the truck till
he knows better. And that's just what I did.

> *Towards the end of this speech* JOE *helps* EDEK *in
> the direction of the truck L. The others follow with the
> rucksack and bundles.* BRONIA *speaks as they leave
> the stage.*

BRONIA (*excited*): It's Jan! He's in the truck! I know he is!
    Stage lights quick fade. Only narrator's spot remains.

Scene 8

IVAN (*narrator*): Joe did not find it easy to persuade the
    camp to take in the family. It was not at that moment
    overcrowded — in fact a whole party of refugees had
    recently been sent back to their countries — but it was
    in a muddle. The Americans were handing over the zone
    to the French. But in the end the muddle helped Joe to
    get his way. It also helped Ruth to get hers.
        Spot centre up. Enter RUTH *from L,* DOCTOR *from
    R. They meet in the spot.*
DOCTOR (*French accent*): I am very sorry; if he is sick he
    must go in the hospital. You and your sister can visit to
    him, but you must stay in the block E.
RUTH: But that's ridiculous. We've travelled eight-hundred
    miles together. I *will not* be separated from him again!
DOCTOR: You must understand it is the rules of the camp.
    I do not make they up, no?
RUTH: That's what they all say: (*mimicking French
    accent*) 'It's not my fault it's ze regulations.' (*Angry*) I
    don't care for your red tape! Either Edek stays with me
    and Bronia, or we're leaving . . . forthwith! (*Turns to go.*)
DOCTOR: Attendez! How you say . . . Hang on. You
    promise you make no more trouble for me, I tell you
    what.
RUTH (*suspicious*): What?
DOCTOR: Maybe I get big trouble for this. (RUTH *forces
    a smile.*) There is one tent, an old one but he keep out
    the rain. I fix it so you stay outside the hospital. You
    come in and out when you want? You hear your brother
    call . . . O.K.?
RUTH (*grudgingly*): O.K. It's better than being at the
    other end of the camp.

DOCTOR: Now I have to go — sort out this mess. (*He turns.*)

RUTH (*gently*): Er, Doctor . . . (*He turns his head.*) Thank you.

DOCTOR *shrugs his shoulders, but smiles. Exits. Stage lights rise.* JAN *and* BRONIA *are gathered round* EDEK *on a camp bed centre L.* RUTH *joins them.*

EDEK: How long have we been stuck here now, Ruth?

RUTH: Almost a month.

BRONIA: Edek says he's better now, Ruth, and we all want to go. Let's get a boat over the water and find Mum and Dad, quickly.

RUTH: It's not my fault, Bron. The camp superintendent won't let us go. He told me the Swiss authorities are refusing to take any more refugees unless there are relatives in the country willing to be responsible for them. Besides, he says he needs definite proof of identity before any arrangements can be started.

JAN: If we had the sword we'd be all right!

RUTH: If it hadn't been for Joe we might never even have got this far.

JAN: It's not fair: we're so close, yet still so far away.

RUTH: Well, I wrote to Herr Wolff for the sword as soon as we got here. He might reply any day. If only I could remember Gran's address in Basel! I'm not even certain they're alive though.

EDEK: Why don't we grab a boat, there's hundreds on the shore, and try to get across by ourselves?

RUTH: It's no use kidding yourself, Edek, you can hardly walk round the hut without gasping. It might be weeks before we could contact Dad. Our best chance is to wait and hope that the International Tracing Service will follow up the Superintendent's letter. He sent them everything I told him.

IVAN (*narrator*): After the disruption of a war, communication is a slow process. The Tracing Service was overworked;

the index of missing children was growing all the time. Each day brought more and more enquiries. (*He takes out two letters*)

"Is my child dead? . . . Our home was bombed while I was serving in Africa . . ."

"My two sons were taken from me in 1942. I heard they were adopted by a German family in Nuremberg . . ." Enquiries like these arrived with every post. But one day, late in the month, the Superintendent called Ruth to his office. His face was grave as usual. Was it good news or bad?

SUPERINTENDENT *is seated at desk C.R.* RUTH *crosses to it.*

SUPER: Good morning, Ruth.

RUTH: Good morning, sir.

SUPER: Now, that sword you told me about, would you describe it to me again, please?

RUTH: Well, it's about so long. Silver blade. Brass hilt. With a dragon on it — breathing fire. That part's damaged. You see it got rolled on in a fight, and Jan used to keep it in a box. He got it from my father. It was a paper knife you see. It belonged to my mother, and when our house was bombed . . .

SUPER (*smiling at last*): I think that you may well be the luckiest girl in Europe. (*He unrolls a small brown parcel on his desk.*)

RUTH *stretches her hand forward to touch the sword. She grasps it very slowly and looks up at the* SUPERINTENDENT.

SUPER: Yes, it is your sword. Keep it. But the important thing is the letters. Both of them were received by the I.T.S. One is from your father, it was written in January. The other, with the sword, was sent by a Herr Wolff, a Bavarian farmer.

JOSEPH *and the* FARMER *step into the spots L and R.*

JOSEPH (*reading his letter*): The last time I saw them was when I left for work that morning. Later, when I returned to the city, having escaped from the prison camp to which I was sent, I heard that they may have been taken away. My house was destroyed, but I have a secret hope they may be living. There was a small boy in Warsaw: I gave him a paper-knife. He promised . . .

FARMER (*cuts in over* JOSEPH): . . . and the small boy, he had a sort of letter-opener he kept in a box. Now as I understood it, these young folk were heading for Switzerland, but they were in such a tearing hurry to be gone, this sword, which I herewith enclose, was left behind on my mantelpiece. I write in hope that it may be of use to you in tracing the whereabouts of these children, and wishing them all good fortune in their search to find their parents. (*Pause*) In all respect and most sincerely, Kurt Wolff. (*A satisfied sigh*). (*Exit* JOSEPH *and* FARMER)

SUPER: I received this information two days ago, but I didn't want to tell you until I had checked it all. You see your father's letter is months old, and I had to get in touch with him. Apparently he's living in Appenzell, just on the other side of the lake — your mother is there too. Here is the telegram he sent in reply.

He offers it to RUTH, *but she is too overwhelmed to be able to read it.*

I'll read it for you: "Will collect children on 23rd at Meersburg by the afternoon boat. All permit arrangements in hand this end. Trust you will sort out yours. Please wire answer." I wish all our cases could end as happily as yours.

But RUTH *is already running to the others. There is a moment's silence, then much riotous celebration by the bed CL before a* NURSE *sweeps across stage with admonishments and a mop, and drives them all outside.* SUPER *packs up his desk with a shake of his head and exits R.*

Scene 9

If there is a break for scene setting, the children may be able to change. If so, RUTH and BRONIA wear cotton dresses, JAN a smart blue shirt, EDEK an ill-fitting formal suit. Exterior, overcast. A series of stepping stones diagonally from down R to up L where there is possibly a low structure to suggest the opposite bank of the stream.

IVAN (*narrator*): So near; so far away.
The water is wide that separates
Father and daughter,
Mother and son.

The day is long that waits
For the last link of the chain
To be completed.

Patience is old,
Old as the hills.
Children are too young
To be so still.

They must go out to meet
Their happiness; they must run
Out to meet their father's boat.

And in the last hour
Is the greatest danger.

Enter RUTH, BRONIA, EDEK and JAN down R, talking as they come.

RUTH: And he was trying to tell me something — it sounded important — but I couldn't hear a word. You could hardly tell it was father. Then the line went dead and that was that.

BRONIA (*animated*): Never mind! At least we know he will definitely be meeting us this afternoon. It's like a fairy-tale. I feel like the Princess of the Brazen Mountains, flying through the sky on my grey-blue wings!

EDEK: You'll have to be careful you don't get your fine wings wet, little Princess: the sky behind that peak looks heavy as lead.

The light is already very green, and fading imperceptibly.

BRONIA: No! No! It can't rain today. Today is my perfect day. I made it up in my dreams all the while we were walking. I know just what it's going to be like when father steps off the boat . . .

JAN: I bet we could see the boat now if we were up a bit higher. I've watched it before. It steams along the Swiss shore before it makes the crossing. Let's go on past that headland over there. We'll get a much better view of the lake.

RUTH: It means we'll have to cross this stream.

JAN: It's only a trickle. Even Bronia needn't get her feet wet.

EDEK: I think I'll stay on this side: I'm out of breath.

RUTH (*kindly*): That's a good idea. Find somewhere comfortable to sit. I promise we shan't be long.

The three hop from boulder to boulder to cross up to L. RUTH *guides* BRONIA.

RUTH (*shouting back*): Edek! Remember that boat we passed, pulled up on the shore?

EDEK: Well, what about it?

RUTH: It's half-decked in front: you can shelter inside if it rains.

JAN has already gone off L and BRONIA *tugs at* RUTH.

BRONIA: Is that the headland? (*As they exit*) Shall we really see Father's ship coming?

RUTH: Well, if Jan says so, I'm sure we shall . . .

All is still for five seconds or so. EDEK *watches them for a moment and exits R. He is worried.*

The light dims to almost black. Back projection: lightning. Sound: rain. Fades in, quick — heavy — torrential. Then confused shouts off.

RUTH: Jan! Jan! We must go back. We must go back to Edek! Where is he?

BRONIA: He's still up there on the cliff! He's crazy!

RUTH: Come on, we've got to shelter! He'll have to catch up with us!

Enter RUTH *and* BRONIA, *seen in silhouette on the far bank; the storm is at its height.*

BRONIA: Ruth! The stream — it's like a river — it's rising! (*Clinging to* RUTH) I don't want to go across.

Pause: they are caught by indecision. BRONIA *is peering towards* EDEK'S *point of exit.*

BRONIA: Ruth! I can't see Edek's shelter — that boat! Oh Ruth, it must have washed out on the lake — it's GONE!

RUTH: He must have been lying in the boat! He must have been swept out on the flood!

BRONIA: Is that it — miles out in the middle? It might be — but I can't see Edek!

RUTH (*in terror*): Where? Where? (BRONIA *points.* RUTH *sweeps the hair from her eyes and peers.*) Yes, I think . . . Oh Bronia, it's disappearing! (*She sinks down with her head in her hands.*)

The final action of this scene is seen by the audience only as black outlines moving against a storm sky. BRONIA *is looking round in desperation. Suddenly she runs to wings L. She emerges backwards, trying to drag a small rowing boat that's really too heavy for her.*

BRONIA: Help me, Ruth! It's our last chance. We've got to get out there. Edek might be drowning in the bottom of that hulk.

RUTH (*turning*): Where on Earth —

BRONIA: It's half full of water. It was just bumping along the bank. There's an oar in there somewhere. Come and help me pull!

RUTH and BRONIA *struggle with the boat. It hardly moves.*

RUTH (*exasperated*): What's got into Jan? Doesn't he care

about Edek? (*Calls*) Jan! Jan! (*Nothing*) Oh for good-
ness sake! (*Pause*) Look, Bron. You start baling the
water out. I'll try to unjam the oar.

    *They struggle to make the boat shipshape as the
storm rises to another crescendo.* JAN *rushes in breathless, L. He throws his treasure-box into the boat and
drags the oar free with* RUTH'S *help. A moment's look
of recognition between the two. Then all three push the
boat towards C and jump in.* JAN *stands at the stern
pushing with the oar.*

    *Lights to Blackout. The storm sounds over the scene
change.*

Scene 10

    *The storm noise fades. Centre spot up: a cabin on the
steamer, represented by two two-tier bunk beds at the
back and the bottom tier of one at the front edge thus:*

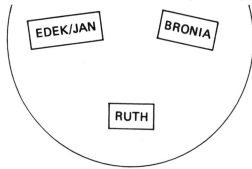

JAN *is lying on his front on the top level of Edek's
bunk. He is chewing on a cheese sandwich and watches
with a kind of detachment, but he should not draw
attention to himself. A crowd of* SWISS PEOPLE *ob-
scures* EDEK *and* BRONIA *who are in the bottom bunks.
They are gathered around* RUTH *who is wrapped in a
blanket. She is waking.* JOSEPH *sits at the foot of*

RUTH'S *bed. He moves to lift her shoulders very gently.*
One of the crowd offers a cup to her lips.

JOSEPH: Feed her slowly. Don't give her too much or she'll be sick.

RUTH (*confused, weak*): Edek! Bronia! Jan!

JOSEPH: Ruth! It's all right. You're on the boat. We picked you up. The storm's gone. It's me, your father. You're quite safe.

At last she realises who is holding her. She struggles to sit upright.

Gently, gently! You've been asleep for quite a time. Try to stay awake and I'll show you what you want to see.

He motions to the people behind his left shoulder. They move out of spot L to reveal BRONIA *asleep in a nest of blankets, snoring gently.*

Nothing much wrong with her!

Again he raises his hand and the same happens R of him where EDEK *is lying, very still.*

RUTH: Is he breathing?

JOSEPH: Yes he's breathing, but only just.

RUTH *struggles as if to get up to* EDEK, *but* JOSEPH *gently restrains her.*

JOSEPH: Edek will need to rest for as long as we can let him.

JAN *gives a stage cough and sits up, swinging his legs over the front of his bunk.*

JAN: They're a feeble lot, the Balickis. They would all have drowned if it hadn't been for me. Ruth, you're crazy. Trying to rescue Edek without my help! You use an oar like a soup spoon, and when a little water comes in the boat you faint. I had to steer out to that wreck of a boat he was clinging to all by myself. I shouted to him, but he'd passed out too. The water was nearly up to his neck. So I pulled him into our boat — two seconds before his turned over and sank.

JOSEPH: You eat your bread and cheese — you need some

nourishment — and stop boasting. If your head gets any bigger it'll explode.

RUTH: You ought to be made an admiral at once! (*To* JOSEPH) Thank God they're safe, all three of them.

JOSEPH: You've got your numbers wrong. I haven't finished yet. Do you think you're strong enough to stand?

He helps RUTH *to her feet. She keeps a hand on his shoulder as they turn towards R.*

RUTH (*as she gets up*): But there *are* only three. What do you mean?

JOSEPH: The last and best surprise. I tried to tell you on the phone but . . .

MARGRIT *has entered from R and* RUTH *falls to her arms.*

Your mother was sitting beside you all the time you were asleep. She slipped away as you began to wake. We didn't want to give you too many shocks at once.

JAN *suddenly slips down from the bunk.* JOSEPH *looks at the two sleeping children and puts a finger to his lips.*

JAN: I wanted to tell Ruth. I haven't got my treasure box any more. I lost it in the storm. I was so busy rescuing Edek. I suppose it's at the bottom of the lake now.

RUTH: But the silver sword! Is that lost too?

JAN (*ruefully*): Everything in the box is lost: two cat's claws, a gold curtain ring, and the buttons off a German uniform. Half a pen nib and an acorn. A stick of Russian shaving soap with some hairs from Ivan's chin stuck in it. Frau Wolff's tin-opener. A silver teaspoon from that house in Berlin — and the brightest feather from Jimpy's tail. They were all precious. I shall miss them . . .

RUTH: But the sword? I gave it back to you, I know I did. I saw you put it in the box and —

JAN (*pulling a long face*): Ah, the sword! (*He looks at*

JOSEPH. *Then a smile of mischief.*) If I'd lost the sword we should never have found you again.

With an air of bravado, he opens his shirt, and there, hanging round his neck on a string is the sword. He lifts it over his head and holds it up to the light, wistful. He turns to MARGRIT.

JAN: This was the most precious of all my treasures. Joseph gave it to me, but it's yours now. (*Pause.*) You can keep it for ever if you'll be my mother.

MARGRIT *holds out her hand to* JAN. *She is too much moved to speak.* JAN *is uncertain. He simply places the sword in her hand and looks blank.* MARGRIT *smiles, takes her arm from* RUTH'S *shoulder to put the sword round her own neck. A glance at* JOSEPH — *sorrow and happiness mingled. She holds out both hands to* JAN. *This time he understands and takes both her hands. She draws him to her.*

IVAN (*narrator*): So the family was united. This is the ending of our story. Be glad it was a happy ending. There were many others which were not. Those who have read the book of 'The Silver Sword' will know there is much we have left untold. They will know too that this is not an end but a beginning.

Pause. Very efficiently the bunks are removed and in groups of two, three and four the whole cast moves gradually on to the stage. Each group is engaged in some building task: measuring, taking levels, humping bricks and so on, in silent mime. The NARRATOR *allows only sufficient pause for his way to be cleared and strolls to centre. Stage lights fade up for him to do so. The cast from the last scene have already joined the others, building.*

IVAN (*narrator*): On a bare hillside in the Swiss canton of Appenzell, a village was built. It was an International Children's village, the first of its kind in the world. Before the war there was only an old farmhouse there, surrounded by fields and flocks of sheep. By 1946 the first house was complete. Joseph Balicki became the house-father. His family grew up with sixteen other Polish children who had not been so lucky. Jan was among them. In Appenzell the building went on.

IVAN *joins the rest of the cast in their building work. There is hammering now and shouting — noise with the mime. Singing too: first a small group, then it catches on, perhaps repeated with the words clearer and a slow fade of stage lights to black.*

Song:
      I dreamt I saw a place
      Far across the water,
      Listening, I thought I heard
      Distant bright laughter.

      Words that I didn't know
      Didn't seem to matter,
      Strangers with willing hands
      Were building together.

      Houses grew brick by brick
      Timber by timber,
      Walls from the broken stone
      Straighter and stronger.

      And as I woke again
      I still heard them singing:
      'This is our starting-place
      Our new beginning.'